Microservice

Architecture

For Scalable Mobile Applications

Microservice Architecture

For Scalable Mobile Applications

Vinu V Das

Tabor Press

ISBN 978-1-997541-07-3

Table of Contents

Chapter 1: Introduction to Microservices for Mobile 8

1.1 Evolution of Distributed Systems in the Mobile Era 8

1.2 Defining Microservices in the Context of Mobile 11

1.3 Common Challenges and Considerations..................................15

Chapter 2: Fundamentals of Microservice Architecture..........................20

2.1 Microservices Principles 20

2.2 Comparing Microservices vs. Monolithic vs. Serverless................25

2.3 Domain-Driven Design for Mobile Microservices..........................28

Chapter 3: Designing Microservices for Mobile Applications..................36

3.1 Service Boundaries and Modularization 36

3.2 Mobile-Optimized Service Interfaces.....................................39

3.3 Data Partitioning and Ownership...43

3.4 Design Patterns for Resilient Mobile Microservices.......................45

Chapter 4: Communication Patterns in Microservices 51

4.1 Synchronous Communication..51

4.2 Asynchronous Communication 57

4.3 Managing Network Constraints and Latency..............................62

Chapter 5: Data Management and Persistence 68

5.1 Polyglot Persistence..68

5.2 Data Consistency Models 71

5.3 Caching and Offline Support..74

5.4 Distributed Transactions and the Saga Pattern in Depth 76

5.5 Practical Implementations and Case Studies 79

Chapter 6: Deployment and Infrastructure.......................................82

6.1 Containerization and Container Orchestration.............................82

6.2 Serverless Microservices for Mobile 89

6.3 CI/CD Pipelines..91

6.4 Multi-Cloud and Hybrid Deployments 94

Chapter 7: Observability and Monitoring 98

   7.1 Logging and Aggregation 98

   7.2 Metrics and Instrumentation 102

   7.3 Distributed Tracing 105

   7.4 Alerting and Incident Response....................................109

   7.5 Special Considerations for Mobile Applications 110

   7.6 Putting It All Together: A Real-World Example...........111

Chapter 8: Security and Compliance 113

   8.1 Authentication and Authorization in a Mobile Context 113

   8.2 Securing Service-to-Service Communication 118

   8.3 Protecting Data in Transit and at Rest 120

   8.4 Regulatory and Compliance Considerations 122

   8.5 Auditability and Logging for Security 124

   8.6 Emerging Threats and Advanced Security Topics 125

Chapter 9: Performance Tuning and Scalability....................127

   9.1 Scaling Microservices for Variable Mobile Loads 127

   9.2 Load Balancing and Traffic Management....................130

   9.3 Performance Profiling and Optimization 132

   9.4 Caching and Edge Computing 134

   9.5 Concurrency and Resource Utilization 135

   9.6 Emerging Trends in Performance and Scalability 137

   9.7 Case Study: Scaling a Social Media Feed Service 139

   9.8 Final Reflections on Performance and Scalability.......139

Chapter 10: Testing and Quality Assurance 141

   10.1 Unit and Integration Testing 141

   10.2 End-to-End Testing in a Mobile Environment 146

   10.3 Contract Testing and API Backward Compatibility ...149

   10.4 Chaos Engineering and Reliability Testing 150

   10.5 Test Data Management and Environments 151

   10.6 Automation and CI/CD Integration 153

   10.7 Real-World Scenarios and Best Practices..................155

10.8 Putting It All Together 156

Chapter 11: Real-World Case Studies and Future Directions 157

11.1 Microservices Success Stories in Mobile 157

11.2 Common Lessons Learned from Real Implementations 161

11.3 Emerging Trends 163

11.4 Long-Term Maintenance and Evolution 164

11.5 Looking Ahead 166

Chapter 1: Introduction to Microservices for Mobile

1.1 Evolution of Distributed Systems in the Mobile Era

The landscape of software architecture has undergone significant transformations over the last few decades. What began as simple applications running on individual mainframes has evolved into vast, globally distributed systems that power everything from social media platforms to mobile banking apps. For mobile use cases in particular, this evolution has been shaped by the rapid growth in smartphone adoption, the increasing demand for real-time features (such as instant notifications), and the need for seamless connectivity regardless of network quality. This section delves into how distributed systems emerged and matured within the context of mobile computing, highlighting the distinct historical milestones that have led to modern microservice-based solutions.

1.1.1 Early Client–Server Models

Early client–server models laid the groundwork for how mobile devices communicate with backend systems. Although smartphones were not yet ubiquitous, the conceptual framework of a "client" initiating requests to a "server" that processes and responds formed the basis of remote interactions. In the earliest days of personal computing, this model was primarily applied within office networks or between desktop applications and centralized servers:

- **Local Clients**: In an office setting, desktop computers acted as clients, each running locally installed software. These machines sent requests to a central server for data retrieval or to perform computations they could not handle locally.
- **Centralized Servers**: The server was typically a powerful machine (or cluster of machines) hosted in a data center. It handled all business logic, data storage, and user authentication. The role of this server was to offload tasks from the clients, enabling them to remain relatively lightweight.

When early mobile devices emerged—such as personal digital assistants (PDAs) and feature phones—client–server paradigms persisted but had to adapt. Bandwidth constraints, limited processing power, and small screens meant that any interaction between the mobile client and the server had to be as efficient as possible. Frequent network disruptions further complicated the relationship, requiring developers to think carefully about data caching and error handling.

Despite these limitations, the client–server model in early mobile applications was mostly a stripped-down version of desktop approaches. The same principles applied: the client initiated requests, the server processed them, and results were returned over some network protocol. However, the volume of requests and data throughput were significantly smaller. This model worked acceptably well for basic features—like text messaging or simple file transfers—but would soon prove insufficient as mobile applications grew more diverse and complex.

1.1.2 The Rise of Monolithic Architectures

As smartphones and their operating systems became more capable, the demand for richer mobile applications skyrocketed. Companies and developers realized that users wanted app stores full of powerful tools—banking, shopping, social networking, and more—accessible at their fingertips. To meet these needs quickly, many teams adopted a monolithic architecture for their backend systems. Under this paradigm, all business logic, data access, authentication, and user management were packaged into a single deployable artifact. This monolith might be a large Java WAR file, a Python Django application, or a .NET solution.

Advantages of the Monolithic Approach

- **Simplicity of Deployment**: Developers and DevOps teams could build, test, and deploy a single artifact. This streamlined many operational tasks, especially in an era when continuous integration and continuous deployment were less common.
- **Easier Initial Development**: For small teams starting from scratch, placing all functionality in one codebase reduced the overhead of managing multiple repositories or complex communication protocols between services.

Limitations in a Mobile Context

- **Scalability Bottlenecks**: As mobile apps gained large user bases, monolithic backends struggled to handle spikes in traffic. A surge in one feature (e.g., a promotional campaign within the mobile app) could degrade overall performance.
- **Slow Release Cycles**: Adding or updating a single feature often necessitated redeploying the entire monolithic application, causing longer QA cycles and higher risk.
- **Tech Stack Lock-In**: Since everything lived in one codebase, it was cumbersome to experiment with new languages or databases. If a mobile feature needed a specialized database for better performance, adopting it meant revising the entire monolith.

In the context of mobile, these drawbacks were especially pronounced. Mobile users interact with apps in short, frequent bursts; they expect near-instant responses, even under less reliable network conditions. The monolithic model began to show cracks under these conditions, highlighting the need for more granular, efficient backends that could scale horizontally and be updated independently.

1.1.3 Emergence of Microservices in Modern Mobile Backends

Following the proliferation of monolithic systems, organizations like Amazon, Netflix, and later Uber discovered that dividing applications into smaller, independently deployable components offered tangible benefits—particularly in terms of scaling and velocity of new feature development. These smaller components, known as microservices, focused on doing one thing well (such as user authentication, billing, or notifications).

Mobile applications were prime candidates to benefit from microservices because:

1. **Usage Spikes**: Certain features (like streaming, chat, or location-based services) could experience sudden spikes, and having them isolated in dedicated microservices made it easier to scale without overprovisioning everything else.
2. **Frequent Updates**: Mobile apps often roll out iterative updates to remain competitive. Microservices allow teams to update specific functionalities without redeploying the entire backend.
3. **Varied Tech Requirements**: A single mobile app might integrate with diverse services—payment gateways, social media logins, real-time chat, analytics platforms. Microservices facilitate selecting the right tool or data store for each domain.

As 4G (and now 5G) networks matured, user expectations for performance soared. Microservice architectures introduced the freedom to deploy services geographically closer to users or to replicate them in high-demand regions, reducing latency. Also, advanced load balancing and container orchestration systems (like Docker and Kubernetes) made it easier to manage these distributed services at scale.

Diagrammatically, a simplified contrast between a monolithic backend and a microservices-based one looks like this:

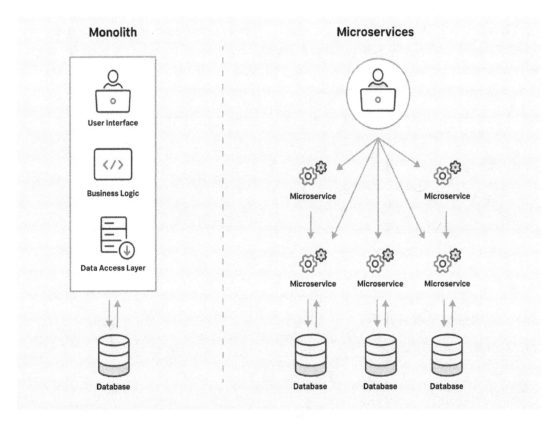

In the monolithic depiction, all functionality is bundled together; in the microservices depiction, discrete services each manage their own data, can be scaled independently, and often communicate via lightweight APIs or messaging systems.

1.2 Defining Microservices in the Context of Mobile

Given the historical background, microservices make more sense when viewed through the lens of mobile demands: lower latency, high availability, frequent feature updates, and user bases that can skyrocket overnight. However, adopting a microservice architecture isn't just about splitting an application into smaller pieces; it's about ensuring that each piece is independently deployable, loosely coupled, and oriented around a well-defined business capability. In the mobile context, capabilities could correspond to user authentication, location tracking, in-app purchases, social sharing, or push notifications.

1.2.1 Core Microservices Characteristics

Core characteristics differentiate microservices from other architectures:

Loose Coupling Loose coupling ensures that services do not heavily depend on each other's internal implementations. In practical terms, Service A is unaware of Service B's internal data models or logic; it only knows a public interface (e.g., REST endpoints, gRPC methods, or an event bus format). This characteristic is vital in mobile contexts since different services may have different traffic patterns. A high read volume on a "content" service should not degrade the "authentication" service. A simple Node.js example can illustrate how one might set up an isolated service (this is a minimal snippet for conceptual clarity):

```
// user-auth-service.js

const express = require('express');

const app = express();

const PORT = 3001;


// Sample route

app.post('/login', (req, res) => {

  // Logic for authentication

  res.send({ message: 'User authenticated successfully' });

});


app.listen(PORT, () => {

  console.log(`User Auth Service running on port ${PORT}`);

});
```

This service focuses solely on handling authentication requests (login, logout, or token refresh). It does not include any logic for billing, messaging, or content management. If you wanted to create a separate service for push notifications, it could be:

```
// notification-service.js

const express = require('express');

const app = express();

const PORT = 3002;
```

```
// Sample route

app.post('/notify', (req, res) => {

  // Logic to send push notifications

  res.send({ message: 'Notification queued' });

});


app.listen(PORT, () => {

  console.log(`Notification Service running on port ${PORT}`);

});
```

Because each service is independently deployable, you can scale, update, or test one without affecting the other.

Autonomy and Independent Deployability Autonomy implies each service manages its own concerns, including data storage, business logic, and possibly even UI fragments if relevant to mobile. One practical advantage is the ability to update, restart, or roll back a single service independently. For mobile applications—where new features or bug fixes might need to be released in quick cycles—this independence is invaluable, as it ensures minimal downtime for the rest of the system.

Decentralized Governance In monolithic architectures, decisions about technology stacks are often centralized. In a microservices world, each team can pick a language or framework that best suits its domain. While this approach requires robust DevOps practices to manage heterogeneous systems, it promotes flexibility and innovation. For instance, if you're building a recommendation engine for a mobile news app, you might opt for Python's machine learning libraries in that service only, without forcing the entire codebase to adopt Python.

Focus on Business Capabilities Perhaps the most crucial aspect is ensuring that each microservice corresponds to a specific business capability. Rather than dividing the system by technical layers (e.g., a data layer or a user interface layer), microservices aim to encapsulate an entire slice of functionality—everything needed to fulfill a particular user or business scenario.

These characteristics become especially important in mobile applications where performance, user experience, and rapid evolution of features drive architectural decisions. If a service becomes a bottleneck—say, the push notification service during a major marketing campaign—you can independently scale it, which directly translates to better user engagement.

1.2.2 Key Benefits for Mobile Applications

Microservices provide several benefits that are acutely felt in mobile app development:

1. **Scalability and Resource Efficiency** Mobile apps often experience bursty traffic. For instance, a social media campaign might drive thousands or millions of new users in a short timeframe. With microservices, teams can selectively scale hot services—like user profiles or media uploads—rather than incurring the cost of scaling an entire monolith. This not only optimizes resource usage but also ensures critical paths remain responsive.

2. **Flexibility and Rapid Iteration** The mobile app ecosystem demands frequent updates. App stores encourage a continuous release cycle, and user feedback can be instantaneous. Microservices let developers roll out updates to a particular feature without risking a regression in unrelated areas. This capacity for rapid iteration is crucial in competitive niches such as e-commerce, where user experience improvements can significantly affect conversion rates.

3. **Isolation of Faults** In a monolithic system, a single failing component (e.g., a memory leak in the order-processing module) can crash the entire application. By contrast, if a microservice crashes, the rest of the system remains operational. Users might still be able to access most features of the mobile app, even if one particular functionality is temporarily offline or degraded.

4. **Technological Diversity** Mobile features can be very different in their computational requirements. A real-time chat service might rely on WebSocket protocols and a NoSQL store optimized for speed, whereas a user analytics service might hinge on big data solutions or data warehousing. A microservices strategy accommodates these differences by allowing different services to adopt the tech stack that best suits their specific needs.

5. **Distributed Development Teams** Many mobile app organizations have distributed teams around the world. By dividing the application into microservices, each team can be responsible for a domain-aligned service—reducing development bottlenecks and clarifying ownership. This approach also fosters specialization; for instance, a team with machine learning expertise can own the personalized recommendation service, while a team with strong security knowledge handles authentication and access control.

By aligning each microservice with a distinct mobile capability, organizations maximize both development velocity and operational resilience.

1.3 Common Challenges and Considerations

While microservices offer strong advantages, they also introduce new complexities—particularly in the mobile domain. As you embark on a microservices journey, it's crucial to anticipate these challenges early. This section outlines two key considerations that often emerge: managing high traffic and real-time data flows, as well as coping with limited bandwidth or intermittent connectivity that frequently plague mobile users.

1.3.1 Managing High Traffic and Real-Time Data

Mobile applications, especially those with a global user base, must handle massive amounts of requests around the clock. Users expect instant feedback, push notifications, and near-real-time updates. A microservice architecture can help by distributing workload across multiple services, but it also means you have to carefully design the communication patterns and the underlying infrastructure to avoid bottlenecks.

Horizontal Scaling Approaches

One of the first strategies to cope with high traffic is horizontal scaling—spinning up multiple instances of a heavily used service behind a load balancer. For example, if your chat service is experiencing a massive influx of messages, you can increase the number of containers or virtual machines running that service. With orchestration tools (such as Kubernetes), this scaling can be automated based on metrics (CPU usage, requests per second, etc.).

Below is a minimal Dockerfile to demonstrate how a simple Node.js microservice (such as the user-auth-service described earlier) could be containerized for horizontal scaling:

```
# Dockerfile for user-auth-service

FROM node:18-alpine


# Create app directory

WORKDIR /usr/src/app


# Copy package.json and package-lock.json

COPY package*.json ./
```

```
# Install dependencies

RUN npm install --omit=dev


# Copy the rest of the application code

COPY . .


# Expose port 3001

EXPOSE 3001


# Run the service

CMD [ "node", "user-auth-service.js" ]
```

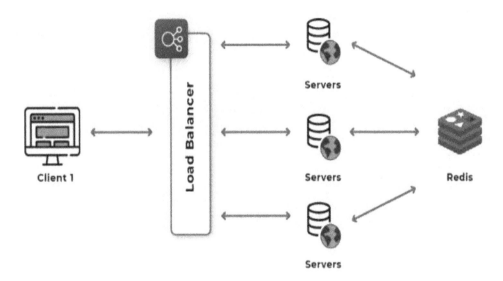

Once the image is built, multiple instances of this container can be launched, enabling the service to handle significantly higher traffic. An example high-level diagram for horizontal scaling might look like this:

Data Partitioning and Sharding

When dealing with large volumes of real-time data—like messages, location updates, or user-generated content—you often need strategies for distributing the data across multiple databases or partitions. For instance, you might shard user data by geographic region, ensuring that queries for European users only hit a European shard. This can reduce latency and also prevent a single database from becoming a bottleneck.

Event-Driven Communication

Real-time systems often benefit from asynchronous, event-driven communication rather than purely synchronous (request–response) APIs. Mobile push notifications are a perfect example: when a user likes a post, the system emits an event ("postLiked") that triggers multiple microservices (e.g., real-time analytics, notifications, feed updates). Such an approach helps decouple the services further because each service merely "listens" for events that are relevant to it.

```
// Example of an event emission using Node.js and a simple pub/sub library

const EventEmitter = require('events');

const eventBus = new EventEmitter();


eventBus.on('postLiked', (data) => {

  console.log(`Notification Service: Send push notification to user ${data.userId}`);

  // Additional push notification logic...

});


// Emitting the event

eventBus.emit('postLiked', { userId: '12345', postId: 'abcde' });
```

While a simple in-process event bus is insufficient for highly distributed systems, this snippet illustrates the basic concept. In production, you'd likely use a message broker such as RabbitMQ, Apache Kafka, or a cloud-based pub/sub system.

1.3.2 Handling Limited Bandwidth and Intermittent Connectivity

A significant percentage of mobile users do not enjoy flawless, high-speed connectivity at all times. Even in developed regions, users may move between Wi-Fi and mobile data, entering coverage dead zones or traveling underground on subways. Designing microservices (and mobile clients) that gracefully handle such disruptions is essential.

17

Minimizing Round Trips

When network bandwidth is constrained, every request counts. Frequent round trips between the mobile app and the backend can quickly degrade user experience. A microservices approach can sometimes increase the total number of requests—if each feature is broken into multiple services—so careful design is crucial.

One strategy is to implement an API Gateway or aggregator service that consolidates requests from the mobile client. Instead of making three separate calls (e.g., for user info, notifications, and app settings), the client makes a single call to the gateway, which fans out the requests to the appropriate microservices internally. This reduces the data exchanged over the mobile network.

Caching and Offline Support on the Client

Offline functionality is a hallmark of well-designed mobile apps. Even if connectivity is lost, the user should still be able to read cached data, queue actions (like sending messages), and automatically resync when they come back online. While this logic primarily resides on the mobile client, your microservice architecture can assist by:

- **Providing small, cacheable responses** (e.g., JSON data tailored for offline storage).
- **Supporting eventually consistent updates** where actions are queued on the device and reconciled later with the server.
- **Offering a delta or sync API** that allows the client to fetch only changes since its last successful sync, reducing data usage.

Graceful Degradation

Intermittent connectivity calls for a mindset of graceful degradation. Features should degrade in a way that still maintains the core user journey. For example, if the push notification service is temporarily unreachable due to network constraints, the user might see a local in-app badge for new messages once the app reconnects, rather than being left entirely unaware of updates.

Below is a small conceptual diagram showing how mobile clients might cache data locally before syncing with microservices:

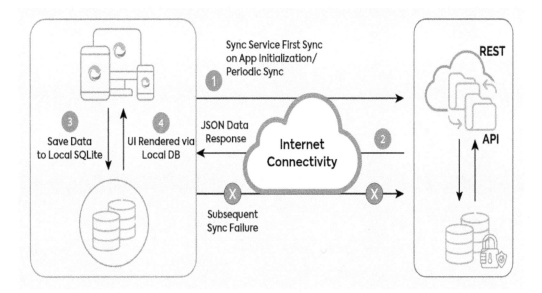

In offline mode, the app relies on local storage. When connectivity is restored, it sends a batched or delta update to the microservices through an API Gateway. This approach helps keep the user experience smooth, even under problematic network conditions.

In conclusion, the historical context of distributed systems—moving from early client–server models to monolithic architectures, and finally to microservices—provides critical insight into why microservices have gained such prominence in mobile. As discussed:

- **Early client–server** approaches introduced basic remote interactions.
- **Monolithic architectures** gained popularity for their simplicity of deployment but struggled with scalability and rapid iteration needs of mobile.
- **Microservices** emerged to solve these limitations, offering benefits like independent scaling, rapid updates, and isolation of faults.

Mobile demands—such as unpredictable traffic spikes, user expectations for real-time updates, and partial connectivity—further amplify the relevance of microservices. Yet, challenges remain, particularly in managing high traffic, real-time data processing, and building resiliency for limited or intermittent network conditions. Strategies such as event-driven communication, efficient caching, offline-first design, and selective horizontal scaling all play a role in ensuring a robust user experience.

Chapter 2: Fundamentals of Microservice Architecture

2.1 Microservices Principles

The term "microservices" may evoke images of small, independently running components, but the concept transcends mere size. Microservices architecture rests on a set of guiding principles that prioritize modularity, autonomy, resilience, and alignment with business capabilities. By internalizing these principles, development teams can more effectively design, deploy, and maintain services that are loosely coupled yet highly cohesive within their domains.

2.1.1 Single Responsibility per Service

A hallmark of microservices is the Single Responsibility Principle (SRP), which states that each service should focus on one business capability or domain-specific function. Rather than structuring an application by technical layers (e.g., UI, data, and business logic all in one vertical slice), microservices revolve around specific user or business needs.

- **Why It Matters**:
    1. **Clear Ownership**: Each team or developer knows exactly which feature or domain they manage.
    2. **Reduced Complexity**: Splitting a large system into small units lowers the cognitive load when evolving or debugging.

3. **Independent Scaling**: Services dealing with high traffic, such as push notifications or data analytics, can be scaled independently without overprovisioning the rest of the system.

- **Practical Example**: Suppose you're building a microservices-based mobile app for ride-sharing. Instead of having a single "backend" that handles user authentication, trip requests, driver management, payment processing, etc., you create separate services:
    1. **User Service** – manages user accounts, authentication, and profiles.
    2. **Trip Service** – tracks ongoing trips, calculates fares, logs routes.
    3. **Billing Service** – handles payment methods, billing cycles, and transaction records.
    4. **Driver Service** – manages driver data, onboarding, and schedule.

Each service covers exactly one major business capability. This segmentation ensures that changes to, say, the billing mechanism, do not spill over into how user profiles are managed.

2.1.2 Autonomous and Independently Deployable Services

In a microservices ecosystem, each service can be developed, tested, deployed, and scaled independently. This concept goes beyond code separation; it implies autonomy of decisions regarding the technology stack, data schema, and release cycles. One service might be written in Node.js while another uses Go if that's optimal for its specific workload.

- **Why It Matters**:
    1. **Deployment Freedom**: Teams can release new versions of a service without coordinating with every other team.
    2. **Tech Heterogeneity**: If a particular domain aligns better with a certain programming language, the service team is free to choose it (though organizational governance may still impose some guidelines).
    3. **Reduced Blast Radius**: A failure or code regression in one service typically does not crash the entire application, improving overall reliability.
- **Sample Deployment Workflow**:
    1. **Local Development**: Each service resides in its own repository, complete with test suites and containerization scripts.
    2. **Continuous Integration (CI)**: On code push, automated pipelines build the service, run tests, and produce versioned container images.
    3. **Continuous Deployment (CD)**: The new container image is deployed to a staging or production environment. Only that single service is updated.

Below is a conceptual diagram showing how each microservice can have its own CI/CD pipeline:

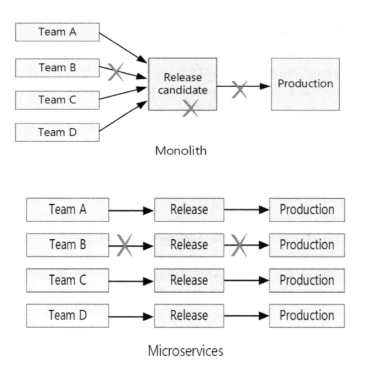

Monolith

Microservices

In this setup, Repository A is for, say, the user-authentication service, Repository B is for the driver-management service, and so on. Each pipeline stands alone, allowing a more agile release process.

2.1.3 Loose Coupling and High Cohesion

Microservices aim for loose coupling, meaning each service communicates with others primarily through stable and minimal interfaces—often RESTful APIs, message queues, or gRPC calls. Internally, each service should exhibit high cohesion, performing tasks that strongly relate to its core business responsibility.

- **Loose Coupling**:
  - **Interface-Driven Communication**: Services do not share data stores or call each other's internal methods directly. They exchange data via well-defined APIs or events.
  - **Reduced Ripple Effects**: Changes in one service's internal logic rarely require changes in another, as long as the interface remains consistent.
- **High Cohesion**:
  - **Single Domain Focus**: All logic related to user billing resides within the Billing Service (in line with the SRP principle).
  - **Integrated Data Management**: If the Billing Service needs historical transactions, it manages its own transactions database.

Below is a small Node.js example demonstrating how a microservice might define a simple

REST interface without revealing internal data structures:

```javascript
// billing-service.js

const express = require('express');

const app = express();

app.use(express.json());


// This route provides a minimal interface for charging a user.

app.post('/billing/charge', async (req, res) => {

  const { userId, amount } = req.body;


  // The billing logic is encapsulated here.

  // External services just call this endpoint and do not know the internal details.

  try {

    // Hypothetical function that handles user billing

    await processPayment(userId, amount);

    res.json({ success: true, message: 'Payment processed successfully.' });

  } catch (err) {

    console.error('Billing Error:', err);

    res.status(500).json({ success: false, error: 'Payment failed.' });

  }

});


app.listen(4000, () => console.log('Billing Service running on port 4000.'));
```

The processPayment function (not shown) can contain domain logic, database queries, or integration with third-party payment gateways. Other services interact with POST /billing/charge but are not privy to how payments are handled internally.

2.1.4 Decentralized Data Management

In many monolithic systems, a single relational database serves all application logic. Microservices invert this pattern, encouraging each service to manage its own data store. This approach prevents tight coupling of the data layer and helps each service optimize storage for its domain. Some services might use NoSQL for unstructured data, while others might employ a relational database for transactional integrity.

- **Advantages**:
    - **Autonomy**: Each team controls its data model and can modify it without having to coordinate a massive schema migration with the rest of the organization.
    - **Performance Optimization**: Choose the best database type for your domain. For example, time-series data might go into InfluxDB, while user records might remain in a PostgreSQL table.
- **Challenges**:
    - **Cross-Service Reporting**: Aggregating data from multiple microservices can be tricky. Often, specialized reporting pipelines or data warehouses handle multi-service analytics.
    - **Consistency**: Microservices typically favor eventual consistency over strong consistency. This can be a shift in mindset for teams used to monolithic transactions.

A simplified diagram of decentralized data management might look like this:

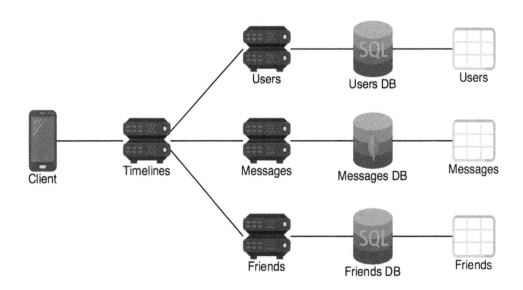

Each service has its own database engine, accessible only by that service. Inter-service communication happens through APIs or events rather than shared tables.

2.1.5 Observability and Resilience from the Start

A final principle is designing for observability and resilience from day one. Microservices significantly increase the complexity of debugging and monitoring since many small services are constantly interacting. Observability includes logging, metrics, and distributed tracing. Resilience involves patterns like retries, circuit breakers, and bulkheads to handle partial failures gracefully.

- **Observability Features**:
  - **Structured Logging**: Each service logs requests and significant events with enough metadata (e.g., request IDs) to trace transactions across services.
  - **Metrics**: Collect real-time metrics (CPU, memory, request latency) and store them in systems like Prometheus or Graphite.
  - **Distributed Tracing**: Tools like Jaeger or Zipkin help identify which service caused a request to slow down or fail.
- **Resilience Patterns**:
  - **Circuit Breaker**: If the Billing Service fails repeatedly, the calling service "opens" a circuit, temporarily stopping requests to give Billing time to recover.
  - **Bulkhead**: Limit resources in a service so a surge in one area doesn't starve the rest.

By embracing these core microservices principles, organizations can build systems that evolve gracefully, remain robust under shifting loads, and align tightly with their business goals.

2.2 Comparing Microservices vs. Monolithic vs. Serverless

While microservices are a powerful architecture, they are not a one-size-fits-all solution. Many applications remain monolithic with good reason, while others might favor a serverless approach. Here, we dissect the key differences, advantages, and limitations of each.

2.2.1 Monolithic Architectures

A **monolithic** application is typically packaged and deployed as a single artifact (e.g., a single .jar file, .war file, or a container image hosting the entire system). Historically, monoliths have been the default pattern due to their simpler initial setup.

Pros:

1. **Easier to Develop at Small Scale**: For early-stage projects or small teams, having all code in one place speeds up local development.

2. **Single Codebase and Build Process**: There is no overhead in coordinating multiple repositories or containers.
3. **Straightforward Testing**: In principle, everything runs in one environment, so end-to-end testing is somewhat simplified.

Cons:

1. **Scalability Challenges**: The entire monolith must be replicated, even if only one part needs more resources.
2. **Slower Release Cycles**: Any change triggers a full redeployment.
3. **Potential for Large, Unmanageable Codebase**: Over time, monoliths can devolve into "big balls of mud," making refactoring daunting.

For smaller mobile applications or products in their infancy, a monolithic approach may suffice. As user bases grow and new features proliferate, however, the monolith often becomes unwieldy and a pivot to microservices might be necessary.

2.2.2 Microservices

As discussed throughout this chapter, **microservices** address many monolithic limitations by distributing functionality across independently deployable services. However, this approach introduces its own complexity in orchestration, monitoring, and inter-service communication.

Pros:

1. **Fine-Grained Scalability**: Each service can scale based on its unique load characteristics.
2. **Rapid and Independent Deployments**: New versions can be rolled out for one service without touching others.
3. **Fault Isolation**: Failures are often contained within one service.

Cons:

1. **Operational Overhead**: More services mean more logs, more alerting rules, and more service-to-service network traffic.
2. **Distributed Complexity**: Ensuring data consistency and debugging performance issues can be more challenging than in a monolith.
3. **Higher DevOps Maturity Required**: Teams need containerization, orchestration, and CI/CD pipelines to handle multiple services effectively.

Microservices shine when the application demands rapid iteration, large-scale user loads, or highly varied domain sub-problems requiring specialized technology stacks. In mobile contexts, microservices help isolate frequently changing features (e.g., push notifications or analytics) from more stable functionalities.

2.2.3 Serverless Architectures

Serverless goes a step further in abstraction. Instead of provisioning long-running servers or containers, developers write functions that execute on-demand in response to events. Platforms like AWS Lambda, Azure Functions, and Google Cloud Functions handle the underlying infrastructure.

Pros:

1. **Pay-Per-Use**: Costs scale with usage, often reducing expenses for applications with sporadic traffic.
2. **No Server Management**: The cloud provider manages capacity planning, patching, and scaling.
3. **Event-Driven Model**: Ideal for asynchronous tasks like image processing, background jobs, or push notifications.

Cons:

1. **Startup Latency**: Functions may experience cold starts, which is problematic for real-time mobile use cases requiring low latency.
2. **Limited Execution Time**: Many serverless platforms impose strict timeouts.
3. **Complex Orchestration**: Coordinating multiple serverless functions can become a tangle of triggers and event subscriptions.

For mobile applications, serverless may be attractive for non-latency-sensitive tasks (like nightly data processing or sending batch notifications) but can pose hurdles for synchronous interactions requiring instant responses. Nonetheless, some teams adopt a hybrid approach, combining microservices with serverless functions for specific tasks.

2.2.4 Decision Criteria for Mobile Projects

1. Scale and Traffic Patterns

- **Low or Predictable Traffic**: A monolithic or lightweight serverless solution might suffice.
- **Highly Variable Traffic**: Microservices or a serverless approach can handle spiky loads better.

2. Complexity of the Domain

- **Simple Domain**: A single monolith might be easiest.

- **Multiple Interacting Subdomains**: Microservices or a domain-based approach typically yield better long-term maintainability.

3. Development Team Size and Skillset

- **Small Team**: Monolith can be simpler to manage initially.
- **Distributed Large Teams**: Microservices can provide clear ownership boundaries, but require significant DevOps expertise.

4. Cost and Time-to-Market

- **Early-Stage or Prototype**: Speed might matter most, favoring a monolith or minimal serverless MVP.
- **Established Product Needing Agility**: Microservices can accelerate new features and reduce risk of regression.

2.3 Domain-Driven Design for Mobile Microservices

While microservices address architectural structure, **Domain-Driven Design (DDD)** offers a powerful methodology for identifying and organizing the business concepts that each service should encapsulate. For mobile applications, where user-centric features evolve rapidly, DDD helps ensure your services align with real-world usage patterns and business objectives.

2.3.1 Key DDD Concepts and Their Relevance to Microservices

DDD, introduced by Eric Evans, is often summarized by core concepts like **Ubiquitous Language**, **Bounded Context**, **Entities**, **Value Objects**, and **Aggregates**. Each concept helps clarify how business logic is structured, making it easier to translate real-world models into software components.

1. **Ubiquitous Language** All stakeholders (developers, domain experts, product managers) share a common language to describe the domain. For a mobile app, this could mean having a clear, agreed-upon definition of terms like "trip," "booking," or "push notification."
2. **Bounded Context** A bounded context is the conceptual boundary within which a specific domain model is valid. In microservices, each service is typically its own bounded context. For instance, the "Billing Context" deals with payment transactions, invoices, and refunds, while the "Driver Context" deals with driver profiles, schedules, and ratings.
3. **Entities and Value Objects**
   - **Entities** have an identity that persists over time (e.g., a user with a unique ID).

- ○ **Value Objects** are immutable and defined by their attributes rather than identity (e.g., a currency amount or an address).
4. **Aggregates** An aggregate is a cluster of entities and value objects with a root entity controlling access and ensuring invariants. For a mobile food-delivery application's "Order" service, the aggregate might include order items, payment status, and delivery address, all managed by an "Order" root.

DDD's emphasis on modeling real business processes resonates strongly with microservices, because each service is a "model in miniature," focusing on one subdomain. This synergy reduces the risk of building "accidental complexity" and fosters a clearer separation of concerns.

2.3.2 Identifying Bounded Contexts in a Mobile Environment

In many mobile applications, domain boundaries can overlap in subtle ways. For example, a social media app may have features for user-generated content, messaging, friend relationships, and notifications. While these features are interrelated from a user's perspective, each can still be a separate bounded context with its own data model and logic.

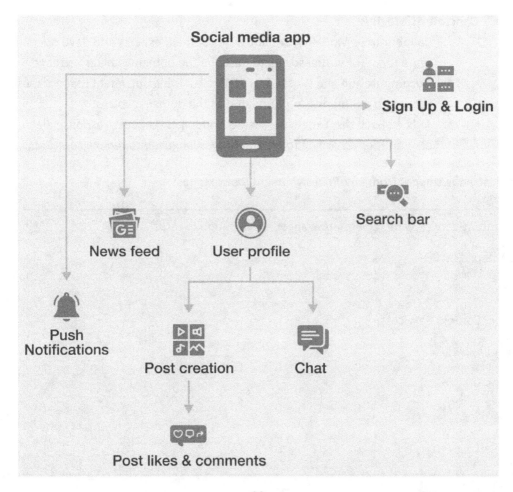

- **Example**:
  - **Messaging Context**: Manages conversations, messages, attachments.
  - **Content Context**: Handles posts, likes, comments.
  - **Notification Context**: Translates events (new message, new like) into push or in-app notifications.

Even though a user may see a post and a notification in the same app screen, internally they are governed by separate bounded contexts (or microservices). The diagram below depicts how bounding contexts might be laid out for a simplified social media mobile application:

The interactions between them (shown by arrows) are typically governed by events or API calls.

2.3.3 Ubiquitous Language in a Mobile Microservice Landscape

Mobile app development often involves cross-functional teams: front-end developers, backend developers, UX/UI designers, product managers, domain experts (e.g., marketing or finance staff). Ensuring consistent terminology among these groups is critical for both velocity and quality.

- **Concrete Strategies**:
  1. **Collaborative Modeling Sessions**: Get domain experts and developers in the same room (or virtual space) to describe the domain in plain language.
  2. **Documentation and Glossaries**: Maintain a living document that outlines core terms and definitions, kept updated as the domain evolves.
  3. **APIs Reflect the Language**: Name endpoints, request/response fields, and data entities according to the ubiquitous language to reduce confusion.

An illustrative snippet from an API design might look like this:

```
# content-service.yaml (OpenAPI/Swagger specification excerpt)

openapi: '3.0.0'

info:

 title: Content Service

 version: '1.0'

paths:

 /posts:

  post:
```

```yaml
  summary: Create a new Post

  description: Use this endpoint to create a new piece of content in the system.

  requestBody:

    required: true

    content:

      application/json:

        schema:

          $ref: '#/components/schemas/NewPost'

  responses:

    '201':

      description: Post created successfully


components:

  schemas:

    NewPost:

      type: object

      properties:

        authorId:

          type: string

          description: Unique identifier of the user creating the post

        contentText:

          type: string

          description: The main text body of the post

        mediaUrls:

          type: array

          items:
```

```
      type: string

      description: Optional list of media attachments (images, videos)
```

Here, notice terms like "Post," "authorId," and "contentText" precisely match the domain's ubiquitous language. This clarity extends from design to implementation, ensuring everyone from QA to product managers understands what "post" means in the app's context.

2.3.4 Aligning Microservices with Domain-Driven Aggregates

Once bounded contexts and the ubiquitous language are clarified, the next step is mapping aggregates to microservice operations. For instance, in a banking mobile app, the "Account" aggregate might handle a user's balance, transaction history, and overdraft rules. This entire cluster of logic belongs to a single microservice if it aligns neatly with a bounded context—like an "Accounts" context.

- **Aggregate Design**:
  - **Consistency Boundaries**: All entities within the aggregate share a transactional boundary. For example, updating an account balance when a withdrawal occurs is an atomic operation within the "Account" aggregate.
  - **Integration via Domain Events**: If changes within one aggregate need to notify other bounded contexts (e.g., a monthly statement aggregator in a different microservice), you emit domain events rather than directly invoking that microservice's internals.

A simple code snippet in a domain-driven style (using TypeScript for clarity) might look like this:

```
// account-aggregate.ts

export class Account {

  private balance: number;

  private transactions: Array<Transaction>;


  constructor(initialBalance: number = 0) {

    this.balance = initialBalance;

    this.transactions = [];
```

```
  }

  public deposit(amount: number): void {
    if (amount <= 0) {
      throw new Error('Deposit amount must be positive.');
    }
    this.balance += amount;
    this.transactions.push(new Transaction('deposit', amount));
  }

  public withdraw(amount: number): void {
    if (amount <= 0) {
      throw new Error('Withdraw amount must be positive.');
    }
    if (amount > this.balance) {
      throw new Error('Insufficient funds.');
    }
    this.balance -= amount;
    this.transactions.push(new Transaction('withdraw', amount));
  }

  // Additional methods for retrieving transaction history, etc.
}

class Transaction {
  constructor(public type: string, public amount: number) {}
```

```
}
```

This Account class can be part of an "Accounts" microservice that enforces business rules (no negative balance, transaction logging, etc.) within its aggregate boundary. Other services (like "Customer Profile" or "Notifications") must invoke APIs or respond to events rather than manipulate the account data directly.

2.3.5 Context Mapping and Integrations

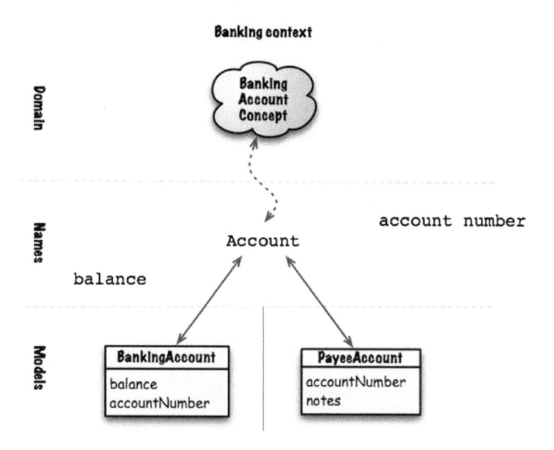

In real-world mobile applications, bounded contexts rarely operate in complete isolation. At times, you need to integrate them. **Context Mapping** is a DDD exercise to document and manage how bounded contexts interact. For example:

- **Customer Profile Context** might publish an event "CustomerDeactivated" when a user closes an account.
- **Billing Context** subscribes to "CustomerDeactivated" to archive or finalize outstanding invoices.

This pattern ensures minimal coupling: the banking context does not rely on internal tables or code from the Payee Account context; it merely reacts to a domain event.

A sample architectural diagram might look like this:

Event-driven integration fosters decoupling and is especially beneficial in mobile contexts where asynchronous flows (e.g., notifications, background tasks) are common.

2.3.6 Advantages of DDD for Mobile Microservices

1. **Clarity in Complex Systems**: Mobile features can accumulate quickly, leading to complexity. DDD's structured approach keeps domains comprehensible.
2. **Evolutionary Design**: As the mobile market evolves, domain boundaries might shift. DDD and microservices both accommodate incremental domain refactoring better than monolithic systems.
3. **Collaboration Between Business and Development**: Ubiquitous language fosters communication, ensuring new features meet actual business needs rather than guesswork.

2.3.7 Potential Pitfalls and Mitigations

- **Over-Design**: Trying to apply every advanced DDD concept from the outset can overcomplicate an otherwise simple system. Start with key patterns (ubiquitous language, bounded contexts, aggregates) before layering on more.
- **Fragmentation**: Splitting the domain into too many microservices can lead to "nano-services," each too small to be practical. DDD encourages a measured approach, ensuring each context is substantial enough to warrant its own service.
- **Misaligned Contexts**: If your domain is poorly understood or in flux, you may define contexts prematurely. Early domain discovery and iterative adjustments help mitigate this risk.

In Conclusion, the principles of microservices—single responsibility, autonomy, loose coupling, decentralized data management, and built-in observability—provide a robust framework for structuring modern applications. A comparison with monolithic and serverless approaches illuminates why microservices are so beneficial for large-scale or rapidly evolving mobile apps, even as those alternatives maintain their own valid use cases.

Chapter 3: Designing Microservices for Mobile Applications

3.1 Service Boundaries and Modularization

Determining the proper boundaries for each microservice is a cornerstone of a successful microservices architecture. While earlier chapters established *why* microservices are beneficial and explored fundamental principles, here we emphasize how to **tailor service boundaries to mobile use cases**, which often differ from typical web or enterprise scenarios in terms of network constraints, user session length, and feature variability.

3.1.1 Identifying Features vs. Business Capabilities

One of the first decisions when modularizing an application into microservices is whether to separate functionality by **technical layers** (e.g., user interface, data access, business logic) or by **feature/capability** (e.g., user profiles, messaging, content feeds). Following widely accepted microservices best practices, most teams have found that **business capabilities** or **feature-oriented** boundaries lead to more cohesive services.

- **Mobile-Specific Rationale**:
    - Mobile features often revolve around a distinct user experience flow (e.g., "Order Food," "Schedule a Ride," "Send a Message," "Watch a Video"). Designing microservices around these high-level features ensures that each service corresponds to a clear user journey.

o Frequent updates to a feature can be isolated within its own service boundary, accelerating iteration without risking regressions in unrelated areas.

Example: A Fitness Tracking Application

Consider a mobile fitness-tracking app that has multiple user-facing features:

- **Workout Service**: Manages workout sessions, including routes, durations, and exercise statistics.
- **Nutrition Service**: Handles meal planning, calorie tracking, and nutritional advice.
- **Social/Sharing Service**: Facilitates sharing workouts or achievements with friends, plus follow/unfollow functionality.
- **Push Notification Service**: Sends alerts for workout reminders, achievements, or friend requests.

Each of these services addresses a distinct capability. If the development team needs to release a new type of workout plan, they can update the **Workout Service** in isolation. The **Nutrition Service** remains unaffected, thereby reducing the scope of testing and deployment risks.

3.1.2 Determining Service Granularity

A frequent challenge in microservices is **avoiding extremes**: too few services can lead to a "mini-monolith," while too many can create undue complexity ("nano-services"). Striking the right balance involves evaluating factors such as:

- **Operational Overhead**: Each additional service introduces overhead in terms of deployment, monitoring, logging, and potential network communication. For mobile apps—which may already require multiple services (e.g., user profiles, analytics, notifications)—this overhead can be significant if you slice services too thinly.
- **Team Size and Ownership**: A common heuristic is to align the number of services with the number of development teams. Each team can manage one or more services. If your mobile app is developed by small squads, creating a large number of microservices may quickly become unmanageable.
- **Service Lifecycle**: Features that change at different rates or require specialized scaling might warrant their own services. For instance, a "Notifications" service (likely to handle spikes) can be separated from an "Analytics" service, which might consume more consistent but heavy data processing resources.

Ultimately, **cohesion** is the guiding principle: each service should handle all responsibilities for its domain (e.g., data schemas, business rules, external integrations) without leaking them to other services. High-level domain modeling techniques (often referencing ideas from Chapter 2 on Domain-Driven Design) help ensure each service boundary encapsulates a coherent set of use cases.

3.1.3 Cross-Service Coordination Patterns

When features in a mobile app span multiple services, you need well-defined **coordination patterns** to preserve a seamless user experience:

1. **Orchestration**: A central coordinator (e.g., an "API Gateway" or aggregator service) handles calls to multiple microservices on behalf of the mobile client, then returns a combined response. This pattern works well if the mobile client needs data from multiple services in a single screen load.
2. **Choreography**: Microservices publish domain events (e.g., "UserSignedUp", "WorkoutCompleted"). Other services subscribe to events relevant to them, reacting asynchronously. This pattern decouples services at the cost of eventual consistency—well-suited for background or offline tasks in mobile contexts.

Example: Aggregator Pattern for a Social Media Feed

To render a main feed in a social media app, the mobile client might need:

*   Recent posts from the **Content Service**
*   Friend activity from the **Social Graph Service**
*   Recommendation data from the **Analytics/Recommendation Service**

Rather than requiring the mobile app to make three separate network calls (which increases latency and data usage), the system can include an **aggregator service** that orchestrates calls to these three services and merges the results into a single payload. This aggregator then returns a unified JSON response to the mobile client.

This approach lightens the mobile network load, essential for preserving performance under variable connectivity conditions.

3.1.4 Modularization of Reusable Components

Mobile apps often share common infrastructure needs across multiple features or microservices, such as:

*   **Authentication Libraries**
*   **Database Connectivity Modules**
*   **Logging/Telemetry**
*   **Feature Flags**

Rather than duplicating these components in each microservice, teams often maintain a set of **shared libraries** in internal repositories. However, be cautious not to reintroduce tight coupling: these shared libraries should address generic cross-cutting concerns without embedding domain-specific logic. Version management is also crucial to ensure that changes in a shared library do not break dependent services unexpectedly.

3.2 Mobile-Optimized Service Interfaces

How your microservices expose functionality to mobile clients can heavily influence the user experience. Mobile environments are characterized by limited bandwidth, higher latency (especially on cellular networks), and frequent offline scenarios. Crafting **mobile-optimized APIs** is thus vital.

3.2.1 REST, GraphQL, and gRPC for Mobile

Mobile applications traditionally interact with backend services via **RESTful** APIs. However, alternative protocols and query languages like **GraphQL** and **gRPC** may offer advantages under certain conditions.

RESTful APIs

- **Strengths**:
  - Widely adopted and understood.
  - Simple to cache at multiple layers.
  - Well-supported by standard libraries and tools.
- **Potential Drawbacks for Mobile**:
  - Over-fetching: The client may receive more data than it needs, increasing bandwidth usage.
  - Under-fetching: The client might have to make multiple calls to assemble all required data for a single screen.

A typical REST endpoint might look like:

```
GET /api/v1/users/{userId}/profile

Host: user-service.example.com


Response:

{

  "userId": "123",

  "name": "Alice",
```

```
"profilePictureUrl": "https://cdn.example.com/avatars/123.png",

"bio": "Mobile Microservices Enthusiast"

}
```

For mobile clients, optimizing the payload structure (e.g., removing unnecessary fields or compressing the response) can significantly improve performance.

GraphQL

- **Strengths**:
  - Allows clients to request exactly the data they need, minimizing over-fetching.
  - Facilitates retrieving nested resources in a single query, reducing round trips.
- **Potential Drawbacks**:
  - More complex setup and learning curve compared to plain REST.
  - Caching can be trickier, though GraphQL clients (like Apollo) offer caching mechanisms.

Example: GraphQL Query for User Profile and Recent Posts

```
query {
  user(id: "123") {
    name
    profilePictureUrl
    recentPosts(limit: 5) {
      content
      timestamp
    }
  }
}
```

Result: Only the specified fields (name, profilePictureUrl, content, timestamp) are returned, eliminating extraneous data. For mobile networks, this can be a significant boon.

gRPC

- **Strengths**:
  - Uses efficient binary encoding (Protocol Buffers), which can be faster and lighter than JSON.
  - Can support streaming, which might be beneficial for real-time updates in mobile contexts (e.g., live location tracking).
- **Potential Drawbacks**:
  - More suitable for service-to-service communication than direct mobile-to-backend calls, due to limited native support in many mobile platforms.
  - Requires additional tooling to generate client stubs (though iOS and Android support has been improving).

While gRPC can be an excellent choice for internal communication between microservices, many mobile teams still expose REST or GraphQL to the client due to broader support and simpler debugging.

3.2.2 Minimizing Round Trips

Minimizing the number of network requests is critical for mobile applications, as each round trip can be expensive in terms of battery usage, latency, and potential data fees. Here are common patterns:

1. **Batching Requests**: Combine multiple operations or queries into a single request. An aggregator (introduced earlier) can orchestrate calls to multiple microservices.
2. **Composite Endpoints**: Offer endpoints specifically tailored to mobile screens. For instance, a "Home Screen Endpoint" that returns user info, notifications, and recommended content in one payload.
3. **Lazy Loading**: For large data sets (e.g., user's infinite scroll feed), fetch data in pages only when the user scrolls, rather than loading it all at once.

Below is a simplified code snippet for an "Aggregator Service" endpoint in Node.js that merges responses from two separate microservices:

```
// aggregator-service.js

const express = require('express');

const axios = require('axios');

const app = express();


app.get('/mobile-home', async (req, res) => {
```

```
try {

  const [userRes, contentRes] = await Promise.all([

   axios.get('http://user-service:3000/user-info', { params: { userId: req.query.userId } }),

   axios.get('http://content-service:3001/latest-content')

  ]);


  res.json({

   userInfo: userRes.data,

   latestContent: contentRes.data

  });

 } catch (err) {

  console.error('Aggregator Error:', err);

  res.status(500).json({ error: 'Failed to aggregate data' });

  }

});


app.listen(3002, () => console.log('Aggregator Service running on port 3002.'));
```

When the **mobile client** calls GET /mobile-home?userId=123, it receives user information (from user-service) and the latest content (from content-service) in a single round trip.

3.2.3 Versioning Strategies for Rapidly Evolving Mobile APIs

Mobile clients often lag behind the newest server versions, either due to users not upgrading or app store submission delays. Therefore, robust **API versioning** is essential.

- **URL Versioning**: e.g., /api/v2/users for the newer version. This is straightforward but can fragment your codebase if not managed carefully.
- **Header-Based Versioning**: e.g., clients include an Accept: application/vnd.example.v2+json header. This can be more flexible but requires a well-defined approach for each version increment.

- **GraphQL Schema Versioning**: Mark old fields as deprecated, remove them in subsequent versions, and coordinate with mobile app releases.

In any approach, define a **deprecation policy**: once an API version is superseded, maintain it for a predetermined period (e.g., 6–12 months) so that older mobile clients can still function.

3.2.4 Handling Offline and Partial Connectivity

Because mobile connectivity is unpredictable, design your microservice interfaces to gracefully handle offline or partially connected states. While offline logic typically belongs in the **client** (via local storage and background sync), the server side should support:

- **Client-Generated IDs**: Let the client create a temporary ID (e.g., a UUID) for new objects, which the server later reconciles. This approach enables offline creation of resources that are synced later with the same ID.
- **Replay Mechanisms**: The server can handle repeated requests for the same operation (e.g., "create post"), ignoring duplicates if the ID is the same. This idempotency design avoids double-charging or double-posting.
- **Delta Sync Endpoints**: Provide endpoints that allow clients to fetch only the changes since their last sync timestamp. This conserves bandwidth and speeds up synchronization.

3.3 Data Partitioning and Ownership

In microservices, each service typically manages its own **data**. This decentralization is crucial for maintaining autonomy, but it also introduces complexities in a mobile environment. Users often want to see integrated views (e.g., order history plus recommended products, or combined chat and notifications), which forces careful coordination across multiple data silos.

3.3.1 Splitting Data Across Multiple Services

Each microservice may have a dedicated database (relational, NoSQL, or otherwise) containing only the data relevant to its domain. For instance, an e-commerce app might include:

- **Catalog Service Database**: Product listings, SKUs, categories.
- **Order Service Database**: Orders, payments, shipping addresses.
- **User Profile Database**: Personal details, preferences, account settings.

This approach isolates changes to each service's schema, but the challenge arises when a mobile screen requires data from multiple domains. Solutions to this issue include **API composition** (using aggregators or gateways) or **replicating certain read-only data** across services.

Example: Catalog and Order Data

A user's mobile "Order History" page might show product names, images, and order statuses. One approach is:

1. The mobile client requests order history from the **Order Service**.
2. The Order Service responds with the relevant order metadata (order ID, product IDs, order date, status).
3. The mobile client (or an aggregator) calls the **Catalog Service** to fetch product details like name and image.
4. The combined data is presented to the user.

Alternatively, to reduce calls, the **Order Service** might store a few essential product fields (like name, thumbnail URL) within each order record, effectively duplicating a small subset of data from the Catalog Service. This trade-off improves performance at the cost of potential data staleness (e.g., if the product name changes).

3.3.2 Strategies for Shared vs. Private Datastores

A fundamental microservices principle is that each service owns its data. However, there are situations where multiple services need read access to the same dataset. Options include:

- **Database per Service**: Each microservice has its own instance, with no direct sharing. Other services must call APIs to access data.
- **Database Schema per Service**: A single physical database is divided into schemas or tables per service. This approach can simplify infrastructure but risks accidental coupling if developers bypass API boundaries.
- **Data Mesh or Data Lake** (in large organizations): Some teams produce "data products" that others can consume. This is more advanced and typically involves a governance model to maintain autonomy.

For mobile apps with moderate scale, the simplest approach is usually "Database per Service" for truly unique data, plus well-defined **API calls** for cross-service access. Over time, advanced data replication strategies might be added to handle performance or availability challenges.

3.3.3 Handling User Data Ownership in Mobile Contexts

Mobile apps typically revolve around user-centric data (profiles, preferences, usage statistics). Who "owns" the user data? Should it live in a single "User Service," or be partitioned across multiple domains?

- **Centralized Profile Service**: Stores essential user info (username, email, hashed password). Other services reference the user by ID.

- **Extended Attributes**: Domain-specific services keep their specialized user attributes. For instance, the "Billing Service" stores payment methods, while the "Rewards Service" stores loyalty points.
- **Global Identifiers**: A globally unique user ID is used across services, but each domain decides which user attributes it needs to store locally.

This structure ensures a user's identity remains consistent, while domain-specific data is owned by the relevant service. For example, the "Social Graph Service" tracks friendships or follows, whereas the "Notification Service" tracks device tokens. Each service can scale or evolve independently without entangling the entire user record.

3.3.4 Eventual Consistency in Mobile Microservices

With distributed data, strong consistency is often expensive or impractical. Instead, mobile microservices typically embrace **eventual consistency**: after a change, relevant data across services will converge to a consistent state, though not necessarily instantaneously.

- **Event-Driven Updates**: A "PaymentProcessed" event notifies the "Order Service" to mark an order as paid, the "Loyalty Service" to grant points, and the "Notification Service" to send a receipt.
- **User Experience Consideration**: If a mobile user triggers an event (e.g., completes a purchase) and then immediately checks their loyalty points, the updated points might not appear instantly. The UI can display a spinner or a note indicating the update is in progress.

Because mobile users may be offline, the system must also handle **delayed user actions**. When the user reconnects, the client uploads queued events that might be processed after other system changes have occurred, necessitating conflict resolution logic on the server side.

3.4 Design Patterns for Resilient Mobile Microservices

Mobile environments can be unforgiving. Latency spikes, packet loss, and ephemeral connections can wreak havoc on microservices if they are not designed with resilience in mind. This section covers **commonly used patterns** that fortify microservices against the demands of mobile traffic.

3.4.1 Circuit Breakers and Retry Policies

When one service calls another, the second service might be slow or unavailable. Without protective measures, repeated failed attempts can cause cascading failures. The **circuit**

breaker pattern detects repeated timeouts or errors, then **opens** the circuit, temporarily blocking further requests to the failing service and returning a fallback response or an error message immediately.

- **In a Mobile Context**: If the "Recommendation Service" is offline, the aggregator can use a circuit breaker to skip the recommendation call, returning just the user's feed. This approach avoids blocking the entire user experience.

Example: Circuit Breaker Implementation in Node.js (Using a Library)

```javascript
const { CircuitBreaker } = require('opossum');

const axios = require('axios');


// Define the function we want to protect with a circuit breaker

async function getRecommendations(userId) {

  return axios.get(`http://recommendation-service/recommend?userId=${userId}`);

}


// Configure the circuit breaker

const breakerOptions = {

  timeout: 3000, // 3-second timeout

  errorThresholdPercentage: 50, // Open circuit if 50% of calls fail

  resetTimeout: 10000 // Try again after 10 seconds

};

const recommendationBreaker = new CircuitBreaker(getRecommendations, breakerOptions);


// Fallback function

recommendationBreaker.fallback(() => {

  return { data: { recommendations: [] } }; // Return empty recommendations

});
```

```
module.exports = recommendationBreaker;
```

With this setup, the aggregator or gateway will not keep hammering an unresponsive or slow "Recommendation Service." Instead, it returns a graceful fallback (e.g., an empty list) after a configurable number of failures.

Retry Policies

Mobile networks can drop packets or experience transient outages. A **retry policy** ensures that failed requests are retried a few times with exponential backoff before giving up. Overly aggressive retries, however, risk **amplifying** traffic surges, so be sure to implement backoff and jitter techniques.

3.4.2 Bulkhead Isolation for High-Demand Mobile Features

The **bulkhead pattern** isolates service resources—like threads, connections, or CPU usage—so a spike in one area does not degrade the entire system. For example, if your "Live Streaming Service" experiences a massive load, the "Payment Service" should remain responsive, preventing global meltdown.

- **Implementation**:
  - **Separate Thread Pools** or **Separate Container Instances** for each service (or even each endpoint).
  - **Resource Quotas**: e.g., limit concurrency to 50 requests per second for a non-critical feature.

Diagrammatically, bulkhead isolation might look like this:

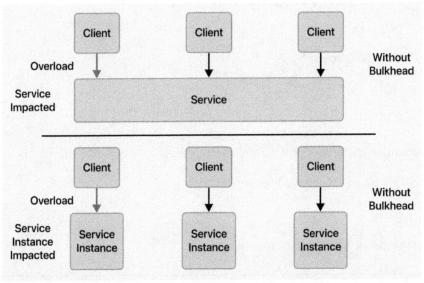

When concurrency in the first service instance is maxed out, the other service instances remain unaffected.

3.4.3 Caching and CDN Strategies

Mobile apps often display repeat data: user profiles, frequently accessed images, or trending news. **Caching** reduces both server load and network usage.

- **Client-Side Caching**: The mobile app can store data in local databases (SQLite on Android/iOS, or specialized solutions like Realm). When the user next opens the app, a local cache is displayed immediately, improving perceived performance.
- **CDN Offloading**: Large static assets (images, videos) can be served through a Content Delivery Network. Although not strictly a microservice design issue, using a CDN can drastically reduce microservices' bandwidth demands.
- **Microservice-Level Caching**: Services might cache frequently accessed data in Redis or Memcached. For example, user profile lookups may be cached to avoid repeated database queries.

A simplified code example for a microservice-level Redis cache:

```
const redis = require('redis');

const client = redis.createClient();


async function getUserProfile(userId) {

// First try to get data from cache

const cachedProfile = await client.getAsync(`user-profile:${userId}`);

if (cachedProfile) {

  return JSON.parse(cachedProfile);

}


// If not found in cache, query the database

const profile = await db.getUserProfile(userId);


// Store in Redis with a TTL of 30 seconds
```

```
await client.setAsync(`user-profile:${userId}`, JSON.stringify(profile), 'EX', 30);


return profile;

}
```

With this approach, repeated calls for the same profile within 30 seconds are served from Redis, drastically reducing database load. In a mobile scenario—where a user might open the profile screen multiple times—the result is a snappier app experience.

3.4.4 Asynchronous and Event-Driven Interactions

Event-driven architectures can be a boon for mobile microservices that need to handle unpredictable traffic spikes or background processes (e.g., offline sync, push notifications). By **asynchronously** publishing and subscribing to events, the system decouples real-time user interactions from heavy computations.

The diagram below shows how an event-driven approach might work for an eCommerce pipeline:

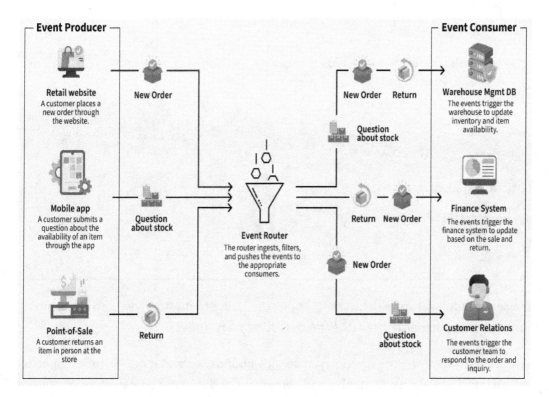

- **Message Brokers**: Tools like **RabbitMQ**, **Apache Kafka**, or **AWS SQS** can queue requests for asynchronous processing.
- **Mobile Use Case**: A user uploads multiple photos in areas of poor connectivity. The client can queue these uploads and send them once reconnected, while the backend processes them asynchronously and triggers notifications when done.

By decoupling the **Event Request Service** from the **Event Consumer Service** through a event broker, each can scale or fail independently without halting the entire user flow.

3.4.5 Idempotent Operations for Reliability

Mobile devices might retry operations multiple times due to intermittent connectivity. The server side should implement **idempotency** for critical operations. An idempotent endpoint returns the same result (and updates the state only once) regardless of how many times it is called.

- **Example**: Payment or order creation requests include a **unique client token**. If the "Order Service" receives the same token again, it recognizes a duplicate attempt and returns the existing order details, preventing double billing.

```
POST /orders

Content-Type: application/json

Client-Request-Id: 9876-unique-id-1234


{

  "userId": "123",

  "cartItems": [...],

  "paymentMethodId": "xyz",

}
```

On the server side, you store the Client-Request-Id. If a request arrives with the same ID, you return the existing response rather than creating a new order.

In conclusion, by applying the principles of **service boundaries and modularization**, **mobile-optimized interfaces**, **data partitioning and ownership**, and **resilience patterns**, development teams can create architectures that simultaneously offer flexibility and reliability.

Chapter 4: Communication Patterns in Microservices

4.1 Synchronous Communication

4.1.1 Defining Synchronous Microservice Calls

In synchronous communication, a service (the **client**) makes a request to another service (the **server**) and waits for a response. During this wait, the client is blocked from proceeding with that particular operation. The canonical example is an HTTP-based request-response model: Service A sends a request to Service B via a REST endpoint, and Service B processes the request, then sends back a response.

This pattern is straightforward and widely used because it maps well to many established web protocols and tools. For mobile applications, synchronous communication can be beneficial when immediate responses are required—for example, verifying user credentials, processing a simple read (e.g., fetching a user's current profile), or retrieving essential data for rendering a screen.

However, synchronous calls also carry risks of cascade failures and increased latency if one service becomes slow or unavailable. When designing synchronous patterns, it is paramount to incorporate mechanisms that avoid turning temporary slowdowns into system-wide issues.

Example: Simple Synchronous Request in Node.js

Below is a minimal snippet showing how Service A (e.g., a "User Gateway" microservice) might synchronously call Service B (e.g., an "Order Service") via HTTP using Node.js:

```
// user-gateway.js

const express = require('express');

const axios = require('axios');

const app = express();

app.use(express.json());


// Endpoint that returns all orders for a given user:

app.get('/users/:userId/orders', async (req, res) => {

  const { userId } = req.params;

  try {

    // Synchronous HTTP call to the Order Service:

    const response = await axios.get(`http://orders-service:4000/orders/user/${userId}`);

    res.json({

      userId,

      orders: response.data,

    });

  } catch (error) {

    console.error('Error fetching orders:', error.message);

    res.status(500).json({ error: 'Failed to retrieve orders' });

  }

});


app.listen(3000, () => console.log('User Gateway Service listening on port 3000'));
```

When the user-gateway receives `GET /users/123/orders`, it immediately makes an HTTP request to the orders-service endpoint (`http://orders-service:4000/orders/user/123`), awaits the result, and then returns the combined data. If the orders-service is slow or unreachable, the user-gateway will block until a timeout or error is returned.

4.1.2 RESTful APIs in High-Volume Mobile Use Cases

REST (Representational State Transfer) remains the dominant synchronous pattern for modern microservices, especially in mobile-friendly API designs. The ubiquity of HTTP/HTTPS support, ease of integration with front-end frameworks, and maturity of tooling all contribute to REST's popularity.

Key Advantages:

1. **Familiarity and Tools**: Most developers and DevOps engineers are well-versed in REST, and an abundance of client libraries and frameworks exist in every major programming language.
2. **Caching Capability**: HTTP caching headers (e.g., `Cache-Control`, `ETag`) can drastically improve performance in mobile scenarios where network calls are expensive.
3. **Stateless Nature**: Properly designed RESTful services do not maintain server-side session state, making it simpler to scale horizontally.

Challenges in a Mobile Context:

- **Over-fetching/Under-fetching**: The client might retrieve more data than needed (increasing bandwidth costs) or not enough data, requiring multiple round trips. Careful endpoint design or aggregator patterns can mitigate this.
- **Versioning**: Mobile apps may remain on older versions, so services must maintain backward compatibility for extended periods or implement formal versioning schemes.

Below is a sample route definition using **Express.js** that employs HTTP caching controls, which can be beneficial for mobile performance:

```
app.get('/products/:productId', async (req, res) => {

  const productId = req.params.productId;

  try {

    const product = await db.getProductById(productId);

    // Example: set a max age of 120 seconds for the response cache
```

```
    res.set('Cache-Control', 'public, max-age=120');

    res.json(product);

  } catch (error) {

    res.status(404).json({ error: 'Product not found' });

  }

});
```

4.1.3 The Role of API Gateways and Aggregators

An **API Gateway** or aggregator service can sit at the edge, receiving requests from mobile clients and internally routing these requests to multiple microservices. While the aggregator pattern was briefly mentioned in Chapter 3 from a design standpoint, here we focus on its role as a synchronous communication hub.

Why Use a Gateway?

- **Single Entry Point**: The mobile app connects to one domain or endpoint, simplifying networking and security considerations (e.g., TLS termination can happen at the gateway).
- **Load Balancing**: The gateway can balance requests to multiple instances of downstream services.
- **Request Composition**: The gateway orchestrates calls to multiple microservices, merges results, and sends a single response to the client. This is particularly advantageous in mobile scenarios where multiple data sources must be combined for a single screen load.

Potential Downsides:

- **Single Point of Failure**: If the gateway is down or overloaded, the entire system may appear offline to mobile clients. High availability setups (multiple gateway instances behind a load balancer) and robust circuit-breaking are critical.
- **Increased Complexity**: Gateways can accumulate logic and risk becoming a "mini-monolith" if not carefully managed.

Diagram: API Gateway in a Microservices Setup

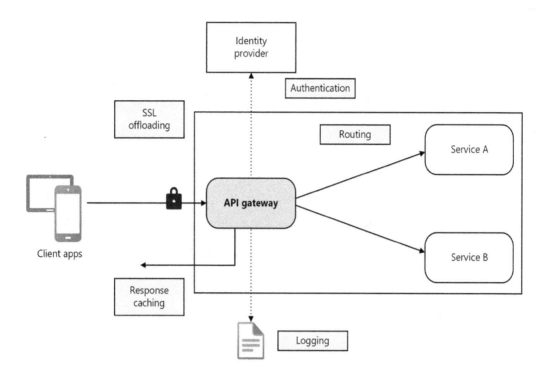

When the mobile app requests a screen load (say /home), the gateway calls User, Order, and Product services synchronously, aggregates their responses, and returns a unified JSON.

4.1.4 Managing Partial Failures

In a synchronous chain of calls, partial failures can cause frustrating user experiences—especially in mobile contexts where network reliability is inconsistent. Strategies for handling partial failures include:

1. **Circuit Breakers**: If a downstream service is failing or responding slowly, the circuit opens to prevent further attempts.
2. **Timeouts**: Each request from Service A to Service B must have a defined maximum time to wait before an error is returned.
3. **Fallback Mechanisms**: If a non-critical service fails (e.g., recommendation engine), return partial data (e.g., user profile without recommendations) rather than failing the entire request.

Example: Adding a Timeout and Fallback

```
// Using axios with a timeout

const axios = require('axios');

const aggregator = async (userId) => {
```

```
try {

  const userProfile = await axios.get(`http://user-service/users/${userId}`, {

    timeout: 2000, // 2-second timeout

  });

  // Additional synchronous calls...

  return userProfile.data;

} catch (err) {

  if (err.code === 'ECONNABORTED') {

    console.log('User service timed out.');

    // Fallback: return a minimal user object

    return { userId, name: 'Unknown', fallback: true };

  }

  throw err;

}

};
```

This snippet ensures the aggregator does not block indefinitely if the user-service is unresponsive.

4.1.5 gRPC in High-Performance or Low-Latency Environments

While HTTP/1.1 or HTTP/2-based REST is the norm, **gRPC** (an open-source framework by Google) offers a binary protocol on top of HTTP/2, enabling efficient data transfers and support for streaming. For microservices requiring high throughput or real-time streaming (e.g., location tracking in rideshare apps), gRPC can outperform text-based REST.

Pros:

- Protobuf-based serialization is compact, saving bandwidth and improving speed—a plus for mobile networks.
- Supports bidirectional streaming, so a microservice and client can maintain a continuous channel of communication.

Cons:

- More complex tooling and steeper learning curve compared to REST.
- Some older devices or frameworks may not have robust gRPC support. However, modern iOS/Android SDKs and cross-platform frameworks (like Flutter) do offer gRPC libraries.

Below is a simplified Proto definition for a user service:

```
syntax = "proto3";

package user;

service UserService {
  rpc GetUser (UserRequest) returns (UserResponse);
}

message UserRequest {
  string userId = 1;
}

message UserResponse {
  string userId = 1;
  string name = 2;
  string email = 3;
}
```

Clients then generate stubs from this .proto file, enabling strongly-typed function calls rather than raw HTTP endpoints.

4.2 Asynchronous Communication

4.2.1 Event-Driven Architectures

Unlike synchronous communication, where one service waits for another to respond, **asynchronous** models allow services to continue processing without blocking. An event-driven architecture (EDA) decouples services via **events**—records of something that happened (e.g., "OrderPlaced," "UserSignedUp," "PaymentProcessed").

Why Go Asynchronous?

1. **Decoupling**: Services do not need to know who is receiving their events; they simply publish. Subscribers can join or leave without impacting the publisher.
2. **Resilience**: Temporary failures or slowdowns in one subscriber do not directly block the publisher. Events can be buffered in a message broker.
3. **Scalability**: Spikes in event traffic can be managed by scaling the broker or the consumer services independently.

This pattern is particularly relevant to **mobile** contexts when dealing with background tasks or intermittent connectivity. For example, a user might upload multiple images on a poor connection. The app could queue them, and once they are eventually uploaded, the backend processes them asynchronously, emitting events for each stage (uploaded, processed, available for preview).

4.2.2 Message Queues and Publish/Subscribe Mechanisms

At the core of asynchronous communication are message queues or topics managed by systems like **RabbitMQ, Apache Kafka, ActiveMQ, AWS SQS**, or **Google Pub/Sub**. These systems store messages (events, commands) until a consumer retrieves them, ensuring reliable delivery even if the consumer is temporarily offline.

1. **Queue-Based** (Point-to-Point)
   - A message queue holds messages sent by producers, and one consumer instance receives each message.
   - Typically used for tasks that need to be processed once, such as generating PDFs, resizing images, or sending email confirmations.
2. **Publish–Subscribe (Pub/Sub)**
   - Producers publish messages to a topic, and multiple subscribers receive the same message.
   - Useful when multiple services need to react to the same event—e.g., "NewOrderPlaced" might trigger inventory checks, shipping label generation, and user notification.

Example: Pub/Sub with RabbitMQ

1. **Publisher (Order Service):**

```
import pika

import json


connection = pika.BlockingConnection(

    pika.ConnectionParameters(host='rabbitmq')

)

channel = connection.channel()

channel.exchange_declare(exchange='order_events', exchange_type='fanout')


def publish_order_placed_event(order_data):

    channel.basic_publish(

        exchange='order_events',

        routing_key='',

        body=json.dumps(order_data)

    )

    print(" [x] OrderPlaced event published")


# Usage:

order_info = {

    "orderId": "ABC123",

    "userId": "user_789",

    "items": [{"productId": "p1", "quantity": 2}],

    "total": 49.99

}

publish_order_placed_event(order_info)
```

2. **Subscriber (Notification Service)**:

```python
import pika

import json


connection = pika.BlockingConnection(

    pika.ConnectionParameters(host='rabbitmq')

)

channel = connection.channel()

channel.exchange_declare(exchange='order_events', exchange_type='fanout')


result = channel.queue_declare(queue='', exclusive=True)

queue_name = result.method.queue


channel.queue_bind(exchange='order_events', queue=queue_name)


def callback(ch, method, properties, body):

    event_data = json.loads(body)

    print(f" [x] Received OrderPlaced event: {event_data}")

    # Trigger push notification or email here...


channel.basic_consume(

    queue=queue_name, on_message_callback=callback, auto_ack=True

)

print(' [*] Waiting for OrderPlaced events.')

channel.start_consuming()
```

Here, the **Order Service** publishes an event about a newly placed order to the order_events exchange. The **Notification Service** subscribes to the same exchange and receives a copy of every message, enabling it to trigger push notifications or other background tasks.

4.2.3 Event-Driven Architectures in Mobile Scenarios

Mobile apps commonly benefit from asynchronous backends in these ways:

1. **Push Notifications**: A user can perform an action (like placing an order), and the system publishes an event that a notification service consumes to deliver real-time updates.
2. **Offline Queuing**: The mobile client might accumulate events (e.g., chat messages, file uploads) while offline, then batch-send them when connectivity is restored. The server processes them asynchronously, avoiding the need for the client to remain connected in real time.
3. **Analytics and Tracking**: Event logs from the mobile client can be batched and published to analytics microservices, enabling near-real-time or post-hoc data processing without impacting the user's primary flow.

4.2.4 Choreography vs. Orchestration

When multiple microservices collaborate to complete a complex business transaction, we often talk about either a **choreography** or **orchestration** approach—both are asynchronous at their core, but differ in how the workflow is managed.

1. **Choreography**: Each microservice listens for events and reacts accordingly. For instance, an "OrderPlaced" event might cause the "Inventory Service" to reserve stock, the "Billing Service" to initiate a charge, and the "Notification Service" to alert the user. There is no central coordinator; the flow emerges from distributed event handlers.
2. **Orchestration**: A dedicated "orchestrator" or "workflow service" receives the initial event (e.g., "OrderPlaced"), then invokes each service in turn (reserve inventory, charge payment, finalize shipping) via asynchronous or synchronous calls. The orchestrator keeps track of the overall process, potentially rolling back or compensating if a step fails.

Trade-Offs:

- **Choreography** is more loosely coupled and scales better, but can be harder to reason about when many services are involved.
- **Orchestration** provides a single "brain" for workflow logic, simplifying debugging but introducing a single point of complexity (and potential bottleneck).

In **mobile** use cases, choreography can be appealing for simpler flows that do not require complex rollback logic. Orchestration might be necessary for complicated business transactions (like multi-step financial flows in an e-commerce app) where explicit state management is crucial.

4.2.5 Asynchronous APIs for Mobile Clients

Although event-driven paradigms often focus on service-to-service communication, mobile clients can also leverage **asynchronous APIs**. For example:

1. **WebSockets**: Maintains a persistent, bidirectional connection between the mobile client and a server. This approach is frequently used for real-time features, such as chat or live updates.
2. **Server-Sent Events (SSE)**: A unidirectional stream from server to client, suitable for sending event notifications.
3. **GraphQL Subscriptions**: Built on WebSockets or similar protocols, enabling a mobile client to "subscribe" to data updates from a GraphQL endpoint.

These approaches can reduce the need for constant polling, thereby saving battery and bandwidth. However, they also require careful handling of intermittent connectivity—mobile apps may drop connections when moving between Wi-Fi and cellular data, or when the device goes to sleep.

4.3 Managing Network Constraints and Latency

4.3.1 Minimizing Round Trips in Mobile Environments

Mobile networks often suffer from higher latency and lower reliability compared to broadband or LAN connections. Reducing the number of round trips between the client and the server is paramount to improving user experience.

1. **Request Batching**: Combine multiple operations into a single request. For instance, a "multi-get" endpoint can retrieve user data, notifications, and recommended content in one call, rather than forcing three separate calls.
2. **API Gateway Aggregation**: An aggregator gateway (from Section 4.1.3) merges data from multiple microservices into one response.
3. **GraphQL**: Allows clients to precisely query for the data needed in a single request, avoiding over-fetching.

4.3.2 Handling Latency with Caching and Content Delivery Networks

Caching at various layers (client-side, edge, or microservice-level) is a powerful weapon against latency:

- **Client-Side**: Mobile apps store data in local databases or memory. For instance, if the user's profile changes infrequently, it can be cached for a session or more.

- **Edge Caching/CDN**: Large static assets (images, video) are served from geographically distributed nodes, reducing the distance data must travel.
- **Microservice-Level**: In-memory caches like Redis can store frequently accessed data, reducing calls to databases or external services.

Example: A "Catalog Service" might handle product data for an e-commerce app. With heavy read traffic from mobile users browsing product listings, the service can cache popular items in Redis for quick lookups, drastically reducing round trips to a relational database.

```
const redis = require('redis');

const client = redis.createClient();


async function getProductById(productId) {

  const cacheKey = `product:${productId}`;

  const cached = await client.getAsync(cacheKey);


  if (cached) {

    return JSON.parse(cached);

  }


  // Fallback to database lookup

  const product = await db.fIndProduct(productId);


  // Cache for 1 minute

  await client.setAsync(cacheKey, JSON.stringify(product), 'EX', 60);

  return product;

}
```

4.3.3 Load Balancing and Traffic Shaping

As the number of mobile users grows, especially during peak usage times (e.g., a sale or big event), the system must effectively distribute traffic among multiple service instances.

1. **Round Robin**: Each request is sent to the next available service instance in a cyclic manner.
2. **Least Connections**: Requests are routed to the instance with the fewest active connections.
3. **Weighted Round Robin**: Some instances (perhaps on more powerful hardware) receive a higher share of requests.

Advanced Techniques:

- **Geographic Load Balancing**: Direct traffic to the data center or cloud region closest to the user, reducing latency.
- **Autoscaling**: Monitor CPU usage, queue depth, or response times to automatically spin up or remove service instances.

4.3.4 Resilience Patterns for Mobile Traffic

From a **network** perspective, resilience means coping with partial failures, spikes, or random disconnects.

1. **Retry with Exponential Backoff**: If a request fails, the mobile client (or microservice) retries after a brief delay, doubling each time. This prevents network storms and gives services time to recover.
2. **Circuit Breakers** (Revisited): A circuit breaker in synchronous calls also helps in mobile traffic scenarios, especially if a service is hammered by sudden demand.
3. **Bulkhead Isolation**: Partition resources (thread pools, connection pools) so that a surge in one area does not starve others.

4.3.5 Fallback Approaches and Graceful Degradation

In a mobile app, returning partial or cached data is often better than returning an outright error. For instance, if a "recommendation engine" is down, show the user's main feed without personalized suggestions. If an analytics service fails, simply queue events and send them later. These partial but functional responses help maintain user satisfaction.

Example: If a mobile user opens a "dashboard" screen that aggregates data from three microservices (User Stats, Notifications, and Recommendations), but the **Recommendations** service is offline, the aggregator might respond:

```
{
  "userStats": {
```

```
  "posts": 120,

  "followers": 450

},

"notifications": [

  {

    "id": "notif_001",

    "type": "mention",

    "message": "You were mentioned by userX"

  }

],

"recommendations": {

  "available": false,

  "message": "Recommendations not available at this time."

}

}
```

Although partial, the user can still see stats and notifications. Once the recommendation service is back online, requests automatically include that data again.

4.3.6 Service Mesh and Advanced Networking in Microservices

A **service mesh**—e.g., **Istio**, **Linkerd**, or **Consul**—is an infrastructure layer that manages service-to-service communication. It can handle load balancing, encryption, retries, and circuit breaking, often via sidecar proxies attached to each service instance.

- **Benefits**:
    - **Transparent to Apps**: Developers focus on business logic, while the mesh manages network concerns.
    - **Observability**: Collects metrics and traces for each request.
    - **Security**: Can enforce mutual TLS, rotating certificates automatically.

While not mandatory for all microservices, a service mesh can be especially beneficial in large-scale environments where each microservice must robustly handle ephemeral connections from mobile devices.

Extended Perspectives on Communication Patterns

While the previous sections cover the fundamentals, the complexity of microservices in real-world mobile applications often requires combining multiple patterns:

- **Hybrid Synchronous + Asynchronous**: A mobile endpoint might rely on synchronous aggregator calls for immediate data, but those aggregator calls are in turn triggered by asynchronous event processing behind the scenes (e.g., precomputed analytics).
- **CQRS (Command Query Responsibility Segregation)**: Commands to update data may be asynchronous, while queries for read data might be synchronous.
- **Sagas for Distributed Transactions**: For multi-service workflows (like placing an order, charging the user, booking delivery), a saga pattern can coordinate asynchronous steps and rollback/compensation if needed.

Example: Combining Patterns in a Mobile E-Commerce Scenario

1. **User opens the app** and sees a "Deals of the Day" banner. The aggregator gateway obtains deals from an "Offers Service" synchronously.
2. **User places an order**. The "Order Service" publishes an `OrderPlaced` event to RabbitMQ.
3. **Inventory Service** consumes the `OrderPlaced` event asynchronously, checks stock, and either reserves it or publishes an `OutOfStock` event.
4. **Billing Service** also listens for `OrderPlaced` events, attempts a credit card charge. If successful, it publishes a `PaymentSucceeded` event, or if it fails, it publishes a `PaymentFailed` event.
5. **Order Service** listens for these events to finalize or cancel the order. The aggregator gateway remains largely unaffected by these internal workflows—it just retrieves final order status when the mobile client requests a summary.

In such a design, the mobile client sees near-instant feedback for certain operations (e.g., it gets an order ID in the response). The subsequent steps—charging, stock reservation, shipping label creation—happen asynchronously, with the user receiving push notifications or updated status screens as events are processed.

In conclusion, synchronous communication—commonly implemented via REST—enables direct request-response calls, suitable for immediate data retrieval or critical user actions that require quick feedback. The trade-offs include potential coupling and risk of cascading failures, making patterns like circuit breakers, timeouts, and fallback mechanisms essential.

On the other hand, asynchronous communication via event-driven architectures, message queues, and pub/sub systems can decouple services, scale better, and handle background tasks more gracefully. This approach shines for tasks that do not require instantaneous responses, such as analytics pipelines, offline sync, and post-processing. Architectural options like choreography vs. orchestration further shape how distributed workflows handle complex business logic.

Chapter 5: Data Management and Persistence

5.1 Polyglot Persistence

5.1.1 Defining Polyglot Persistence

In a monolithic architecture, it's common to rely on a single relational database (like PostgreSQL or MySQL) that stores all application data. Microservices, by contrast, encourage **polyglot persistence**: each service uses the database model (relational, document, key-value, time-series, graph, etc.) best suited to its domain. This approach can significantly enhance performance and productivity but requires carefully managing multiple data stores.

Key Benefits:

- **Optimal Technology Fit**: A location-tracking microservice might store user coordinates efficiently in a geospatial database, while a user-profile microservice might prefer a document store.
- **Autonomous Evolution**: Each microservice can evolve its schema or switch databases without impacting the others.
- **Scalability and Cost-Effectiveness**: Services with large write volumes might choose a NoSQL database for horizontal scaling, while smaller services can remain on a simpler relational model.

Potential Drawbacks:

- **Operational Complexity**: Multiple databases mean multiple sets of backup and disaster recovery procedures, as well as different query languages and performance tuning parameters.
- **Data Fragmentation**: Integrating or reporting across services can become more complex if data lives in numerous specialized stores.

For **mobile applications**, polyglot persistence often aligns well with feature-specific performance requirements. For instance, if one microservice handles real-time chat, a high-throughput NoSQL store with built-in replication might be ideal. Another microservice might store analytics data in a columnar database for fast aggregate queries.

5.1.2 Common Database Paradigms in Microservices

1. **Relational Databases (SQL)**
   - **Examples**: PostgreSQL, MySQL, Microsoft SQL Server.
   - **When to Use**: Transactions that demand ACID compliance (e.g., billing, payment).
   - **Advantages**: Mature ecosystems, strong consistency, robust query capabilities (joins, indexing).
   - **Challenges**: Horizontal scaling can be more complex than many NoSQL solutions.
2. **Key-Value Stores**
   - **Examples**: Redis, Amazon DynamoDB, Riak.
   - **When to Use**: Caching layers, sessions, user preferences, or small, fast lookups.
   - **Advantages**: Ultra-low latency, easy horizontal scaling.
   - **Challenges**: Limited query operations, typically best for simple data structures.
3. **Document Databases**
   - **Examples**: MongoDB, Couchbase, Firebase Firestore.
   - **When to Use**: Handling semi-structured data (like user profiles or product catalogs).
   - **Advantages**: Flexible schemas, natural representation of JSON-like objects, easy to replicate.
   - **Challenges**: Potentially inconsistent data if not carefully designed, indexing complexities for queries.
4. **Column-Family Databases**
   - **Examples**: Apache Cassandra, HBase.
   - **When to Use**: High-velocity writes, large datasets, and heavy analytical queries.
   - **Advantages**: Designed for massive scalability, partition-tolerant.

- **Challenges**: Learning curve, data modeling can be tricky, eventual consistency trade-offs.

5. **Graph Databases**
   - **Examples**: Neo4j, Amazon Neptune.
   - **When to Use**: Social graphs, recommendation engines, and other highly connected data sets.
   - **Advantages**: Direct modeling of relationships, fast traversals.
   - **Challenges**: Niche use cases, potentially unfamiliar query languages (e.g., Cypher, Gremlin).

6. **Time-Series Databases**
   - **Examples**: InfluxDB, TimescaleDB.
   - **When to Use**: Metrics, logs, sensor data, real-time analytics, usage patterns.
   - **Advantages**: Optimized for time-based queries and retention policies.
   - **Challenges**: Limited in domain scope if you also need relational or complex operations.

Diagram: Example Polyglot Persistence in a Mobile/Web Ecosystem

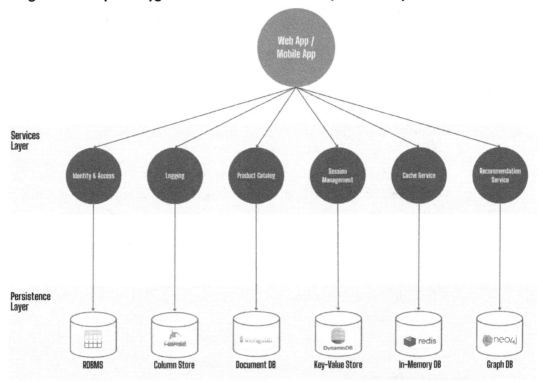

In this hypothetical scenario, each microservice chooses a database aligned with its domain needs.

5.1.3 Data Partitioning and Sharding

Even within a single microservice, you may need to **partition** or **shard** data for scalability and latency optimization. Partitioning splits data across multiple nodes based on certain partition keys (e.g., user ID, region, or order ID range). Sharding is particularly critical in global mobile applications where user traffic can spike in localized areas or at certain times.

- **Horizontal Sharding**: Distribute rows of a table across multiple servers or clusters.
- **Vertical Sharding**: Separate columns or feature sets across different databases (less common in microservices, but used if certain attributes are rarely accessed and can reside in a separate store).
- **Geo-Sharding**: Place data in servers geographically close to the user. Typically used to reduce latency in global apps or comply with data sovereignty laws (e.g., GDPR in the EU).

Example: An e-commerce microservice that sees a large portion of traffic from Asia might place user data for Asian customers in an Asia-based data center, while data for North American customers resides in a North American data center. The microservice's logic determines which shard to query based on user ID or region.

5.1.4 Managing Schema Changes

In a monolithic setting, schema changes often involve global migrations, potentially causing downtime. Microservices allow each service to evolve its schema independently, but teams still need a safe approach to rolling out changes—especially for mobile applications that could have older clients.

- **Backward Compatibility**: Introduce new fields or tables in a way that older versions of the service can still process data.
- **Zero-Downtime Migrations**: Phase in new schemas, keep both old and new columns/tables for a transition period, then remove the old only after confirming no references remain.
- **Evolutionary Database Design**: Tools like **Flyway** or **Liquibase** for relational databases help version migrations. For NoSQL, tracking schema evolution in code (e.g., versioned schema definitions) is common.

5.2 Data Consistency Models

5.2.1 The CAP Theorem in the Microservices World

The **CAP theorem** states that a distributed system can only provide two out of three guarantees: **Consistency**, **Availability**, and **Partition tolerance**. Partition tolerance is a given in microservices that might span data centers or cloud regions. Thus, architects must choose between stronger consistency or better availability in the face of network partitions. This trade-off profoundly influences data design and user experience in mobile apps.

1. **CP (Consistency + Partition Tolerance)**: The system sacrifices availability under partition but keeps data globally consistent. For example, if a single partition becomes unreachable, that part of the system may block or reject writes to avoid inconsistency.
2. **AP (Availability + Partition Tolerance)**: The system stays up and responsive even if partitions occur, but data might become temporarily inconsistent, reconciling itself eventually.

Many microservices adopt **AP** properties for high availability, especially in global mobile contexts where network disruptions are common. However, certain domains—like financial transactions—may lean toward **CP** to guarantee correctness over always-on availability.

5.2.2 Strong vs. Eventual Consistency

Strong Consistency ensures that reads immediately reflect the most recent write. This is straightforward in a single relational database but can be difficult to achieve in a distributed environment where data is replicated.

- **Pros**: Simplifies application logic because the client always sees the latest state.
- **Cons**: Higher latency, potential blocking in the event of replication delays or network partitions.

Eventual Consistency means that after a write, it may take some time for all nodes (or all services) to see the same value. Meanwhile, reads might return stale data.

- **Pros**: Highly scalable, reduced blocking, more tolerant of network hiccups.
- **Cons**: Applications must handle stale reads and design for asynchronous updates. This can be tricky for mobile apps that rely on immediate feedback.

A **common compromise** is to keep each microservice strongly consistent internally (e.g., by using ACID transactions within its own database) but allow **eventual consistency between services** via events or asynchronous replication.

5.2.3 Handling Distributed Updates

When a user action in a mobile app affects multiple microservices—say, updating user info in the "User Profile Service" and adding an entry to the "Gamification Service"—we must coordinate those writes while preserving consistency.

Options:

1. **Dual Writes from the Client**: The mobile client calls both services. This is simple but can lead to partial updates if one service call fails.
2. **Orchestration**: A dedicated orchestrator or aggregator service receives the update request, writes to each service in a controlled sequence. If one fails, partial updates can be rolled back (though this might require advanced patterns like sagas, discussed later).
3. **Event-Driven**: The mobile client updates one service, which then publishes an event that another service subscribes to. This approach is inherently asynchronous, often leading to eventual consistency.

5.2.4 Two-Phase Commit (2PC) vs. Saga Patterns

Two-Phase Commit (2PC) is a classic approach for coordinating transactional consistency across multiple services or databases. A **transaction manager** asks each participant to "prepare" (i.e., confirm readiness to commit), then either commits or aborts the transaction if any participant indicates failure.

- **Downside**: 2PC can be a bottleneck in microservices because it holds locks and can degrade availability. It's rarely favored in large-scale, highly distributed systems.

Saga Pattern is more common in microservices, especially in mobile contexts. Each local transaction in a saga updates one microservice, then publishes an event to trigger the next step. If any step fails, compensating transactions undo or mitigate the changes from preceding steps.

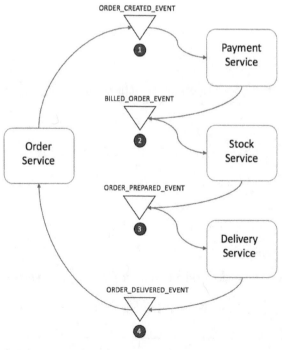

This approach allows partial progress and compensation for failures rather than blocking the entire system in a global transaction. Mobile apps often handle ephemeral connectivity, so asynchronous, decoupled patterns like sagas fit more naturally.

5.3 Caching and Offline Support

5.3.1 Redis-Based Caching Layers for Hot Data

Caching is indispensable for microservices under heavy load—especially when serving mobile clients who expect near-instant responses. **Redis** is a popular, in-memory key-value store that excels at caching hot data (e.g., frequently accessed records, session tokens).

1. **Transient Data**: If losing cached data is acceptable, an in-memory store like Redis offers substantial speed gains over persistent databases.
2. **Session Data and Rate Limiting**: For user sessions or rate-limiting counters, Redis can store ephemeral states that quickly expire.
3. **Geo-Distributed Caching**: In global mobile apps, some setups replicate Redis caches across regions to reduce round-trip latency.

Example: Using Redis for Caching

```
const redis = require('redis');

const client = redis.createClient();


async function getProfile(userId) {

  const cacheKey = `userProfile:${userId}`;

  const cachedValue = await client.getAsync(cacheKey);


  if (cachedValue) {

    return JSON.parse(cachedValue);

  }


  const profile = await db.queryUserProfile(userId); // e.g., from Postgres

  await client.setAsync(cacheKey, JSON.stringify(profile), 'EX', 60); // expire in 60s
```

```
  return profile;

}
```

Every time a mobile client requests a user's profile, this microservice checks the Redis cache first. If there's a hit, the response is immediate. Otherwise, it queries the database, caches the result, and returns it. For mobile apps with large user bases, such caching can drastically reduce database load.

5.3.2 Local Storage Strategies on Mobile Devices

While **server-side** caching is vital, **client-side** caching can also reduce round-trips and mitigate offline conditions:

- **On iOS/Android**: Use local databases like SQLite or libraries such as **Room** (Android) or **Core Data** (iOS) to persist user data.
- **Realm** or **MMKV**: Third-party libraries offering easy synchronization or key-value storage.
- **Web Technologies** (for cross-platform apps): Solutions such as IndexedDB, localStorage, or specialized frameworks (like PouchDB for offline replication).

Offline-First Design: The mobile client tries to fulfill reads from local caches first, updating in the background if the network is available. Writes can be queued locally until connectivity returns.

5.3.3 Handling Offline Writes and Conflict Resolution

Consider a scenario where a user updates their profile while offline—then simultaneously, the user's profile changes on another device that remains online. Upon reconnection, the system must reconcile conflicting writes.

Strategies:

1. **Last-Write-Wins (LWW)**: The latest timestamped update overwrites previous values. Simple, but can lose data if two updates were meant to merge.
2. **Client-Side Merge**: The app merges changes field-by-field. For instance, if the user changes their name offline, but the online device updates their email, both changes can coexist.
3. **Server-Side Merge or Rebase**: The server keeps a record of prior states or versions, attempts a merge upon reconnect (similar to version control systems). If conflict arises, it might prompt the user to choose which changes to keep.

Below is a simplistic approach in pseudo-code for conflict resolution:

```
def syncUserProfile(offlineProfile, currentProfile):

  # offlineProfile = changes user made while offline

  # currentProfile = server's latest known state

  # Strategy: Merge if fields differ, otherwise use server's version


  mergedProfile = currentProfile.copy()

  for key, offlineValue in offlineProfile.items():

    if offlineValue != currentProfile[key]:

      if isMergeableField(key):

        # Attempt field-level merge

        mergedProfile[key] = mergeValues(key, offlineValue, currentProfile[key])

      else:

        # Last write wins for non-mergeable fields

        if offlineProfile.timestamp > currentProfile.timestamp:

          mergedProfile[key] = offlineValue

  return mergedProfile
```

This function could be part of a microservice that handles user profiles, reconciling offline updates before persisting final changes. Real implementations would be more sophisticated, possibly storing multiple versions or using a specialized conflict resolution policy (CRDTs, operational transforms, etc.).

5.4 Distributed Transactions and the Saga Pattern in Depth

While earlier we briefly discussed **2PC vs. Sagas** under data consistency, this section dives deeper into how Sagas handle multi-step workflows for data updates that span multiple microservices. For mobile apps, these patterns ensure a consistent user experience even when transactions are complex (e.g., in e-commerce, a user might place an order, pay, schedule delivery, and earn loyalty points across multiple services).

5.4.1 Types of Sagas

1. **Choreographed Sagas**: Each microservice publishes events when it completes an action. Other services listen for those events and perform subsequent actions. If any step fails, a compensating event is triggered.
2. **Orchestrated Sagas**: A central saga orchestrator (or saga manager) tells each participating service what to do next. If a step fails, the orchestrator instructs previous services to run compensating actions.

Why Sagas for Mobile?

- **Network Intermittence**: Mobile clients may start a workflow (e.g., a ride-sharing booking) but lose connectivity. A saga ensures partial progress is eventually resolved.
- **Complex Business Flows**: Scenes like in-app purchases, multiple shipping options, or user-driven multi-step processes often cross multiple services.

5.4.2 Choreographed Saga Example

Imagine a user in a mobile travel app who books a hotel and flight in one flow:

1. **Booking Service**: Receives the booking request, stores initial booking record, publishes BookingInitiated event.
2. **Hotel Service**: Listens for BookingInitiated, reserves a room, then publishes HotelReserved event. If reservation fails, it publishes HotelReservationFailed.
3. **Flight Service**: Listens for BookingInitiated, reserves a flight seat, then publishes FlightReserved or FlightReservationFailed.
4. **Payment Service**: Waits for both hotel and flight confirmations (or uses partial success logic). If everything is confirmed, charges the user, publishes PaymentSuccessful or PaymentFailed.
5. **Booking Service**: On receiving PaymentSuccessful, marks the booking as complete. If PaymentFailed, triggers compensating actions (cancel the flight/hotel if they were reserved).

Diagram: Choreography Flow

Each microservice acts independently, relying on events. No single orchestrator dictates the entire flow, reducing coupling but making the sequence somewhat emergent and harder to visualize or debug.

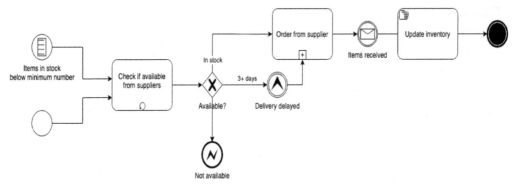

Orchestration - sub-process for restocking out-of-stock items

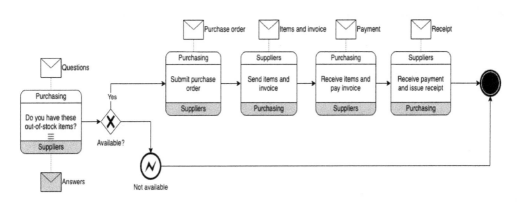

Choreography model

5.4.3 Orchestrated Saga Example

Alternatively, a **Saga Orchestrator** controls the flow:

1. **Mobile client** sends a booking request to the **Orchestrator**.
2. The orchestrator calls **Booking Service** to create a booking record.
3. If successful, the orchestrator calls **Hotel Service**.
4. If that's also successful, it calls **Flight Service**.
5. If all reservations succeed, the orchestrator calls **Payment Service** to finalize. Otherwise, it calls each service in reverse order to compensate.

Example Orchestrator Pseudo-Code:

```
class BookingSagaOrchestrator:

    def start_saga(self, bookingRequest):
```

```
bookingId = bookingService.createBooking(bookingRequest)

try:

    hotelConfirmation = hotelService.reserveHotel(bookingRequest.hotelDetails)

    flightConfirmation = flightService.reserveFlight(bookingRequest.flightDetails)

    paymentResult = paymentService.charge(bookingRequest.paymentInfo)

    bookingService.finalizeBooking(bookingId)

except Exception as e:

    # If any step fails, orchestrator triggers compensation

    self.compensate(bookingId)

    raise e


def compensate(self, bookingId):

    # Cancel partial reservations

    bookingService.cancelBooking(bookingId)

    #       Potentially       call       hotelService.cancelReservation(...)       and
flightService.cancelReservation(...)
```

The orchestrator logs each step's success or failure, ensuring a single "brain" drives the saga. Mobile apps see consistent states as the orchestrator either completes or rolls back the entire transaction.

5.4.4 Best Practices for Sagas

- **Idempotent Operations**: Each service's operation should handle re-invocation without duplicating side effects, crucial if events are replayed or orchestrator retries occur.
- **Compensation**: Plan for partial failures with well-defined compensating actions (e.g., reversing a payment, releasing a hotel reservation).
- **Observability**: Implement logs, metrics, or distributed tracing to track the saga's progress and diagnose issues quickly.

5.5 Practical Implementations and Case Studies

5.5.1 Reference Architecture: Food Delivery App

Consider a **food delivery mobile app** that includes microservices for:

- **User Profiles** (relational DB for user data)
- **Menus** (document DB for restaurant menus)
- **Orders** (document DB or relational DB, possibly with advanced indexing for queries by time)
- **Payments** (relational DB for transaction integrity)
- **Notifications** (key-value store or specialized push service)

Data Interplay

1. **Placing an Order**: The **Orders** microservice inserts a new order record in its store.
2. **Payment**: Once the user pays, the **Payments** service writes a payment record in a relational DB, then publishes an event to confirm the transaction.
3. **Order Confirmation**: The Orders service receives the payment confirmation via an event bus, updates order status to "Confirmed."
4. **Notifications**: The mobile user gets a push alert from the **Notifications** service (which may store ephemeral data in Redis to track active user sessions and device tokens).

In a real-world scenario, the Orders service might also replicate key data from the Menus service (like item names or prices) to avoid cross-service synchronous calls for every order read. This replication is done asynchronously for performance and reliability.

5.5.2 Offline-First Music Streaming App

A **music streaming** mobile app might rely on local device caches and asynchronous sync:

- **Song Catalog Service**: Document database storing metadata (title, artist, album, track length).
- **Playlist Service**: Allows users to create personal playlists, stored in a relational DB or a document store.
- **Offline Playback**: The client caches songs or metadata in a local DB. If the user edits a playlist offline, a local write is queued. On reconnect, the client attempts to push changes to the Playlist service.
- **Conflict Resolution**: If the user also changed the same playlist on a different device, the service merges or prompts the user to resolve.

5.5.3 Performance Considerations

Observations from real-world implementations:

- **Repetitive Reads**: Cache frequently accessed or static data (e.g., top playlists) in memory or at the client.
- **Write Amplification**: If multiple microservices or databases must be updated for one user action, consider event-driven decoupling or aggregator patterns to reduce synchronous overhead.
- **Minimized Coupling**: Let each service own its data entirely, exposing only APIs or events for cross-service communication. Resist the temptation to share tables or replicate large amounts of data blindly.

In conclusion, by granting each service autonomy over its data, adopting the most suitable database paradigm for its domain, and employing patterns like caching, offline support, and sagas, teams can unlock both **scalability** and **resilience**.

Yet, these benefits come with **complexities**:

- **Multiple Databases** demand careful operational oversight.
- **Eventual Consistency** forces new mental models around staleness and asynchronous updates.
- **Offline Support** requires reconciling local device changes with server state.

When done right, microservices can harness data in a way that not only improves performance but also makes the system more agile in responding to evolving mobile user demands. Whether you're building a global e-commerce platform, a real-time messaging app, or a localized content delivery service, the **data management patterns** highlighted here—polyglot persistence, caching, consistent schemas, and sagas for multi-step workflows—provide a robust toolkit to ensure your microservices are truly **mobile-first** in every sense.

Chapter 6: Deployment and Infrastructure

6.1 Containerization and Container Orchestration

6.1.1 Docker Basics for Microservices

Containerization lies at the heart of modern microservices deployments. Rather than running microservices directly on host machines, teams often bundle each service with its runtime dependencies inside a **Docker container**. This approach ensures a consistent environment across development, testing, and production.

Why Containers Matter for Microservices

1. **Isolation**: Each microservice runs in its own container, avoiding conflicts over library versions or environment variables.
2. **Scalability**: Containers can be replicated quickly to handle sudden increases in demand, a critical benefit when mobile apps face traffic spikes.
3. **Portability**: A container image, once built, can run on any host that supports Docker (or a compatible container runtime), simplifying multi-environment deployments.

Building a Dockerfile

To illustrate, here is a Dockerfile for a Node.js microservice (e.g., a "Notifications" service) that might handle push notifications for a mobile app:

```
# Use an official Node.js runtime as a parent image
```

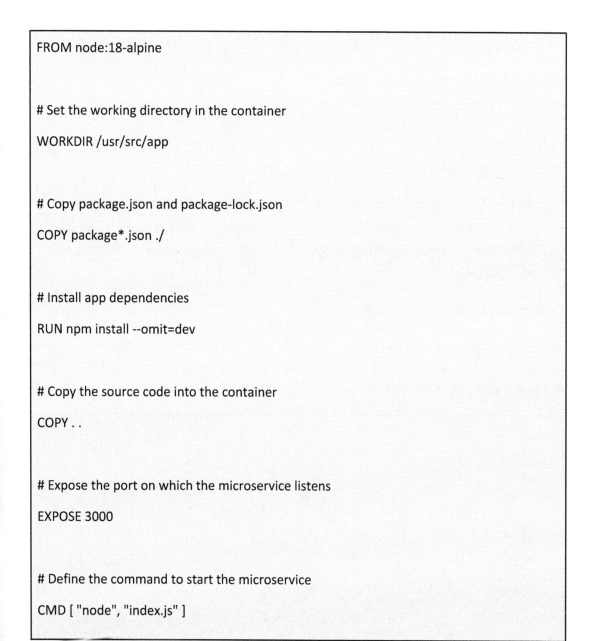

```
FROM node:18-alpine


# Set the working directory in the container

WORKDIR /usr/src/app


# Copy package.json and package-lock.json

COPY package*.json ./


# Install app dependencies

RUN npm install --omit=dev


# Copy the source code into the container

COPY . .


# Expose the port on which the microservice listens

EXPOSE 3000


# Define the command to start the microservice

CMD [ "node", "index.js" ]
```

Key Points:

- **Base Image**: We're using node:18-alpine, which is lightweight and well-suited for production Node.js apps.
- **Dependency Installation**: We install dependencies and then copy the rest of the source code, ensuring that Docker caching optimizes build times.
- **Port Exposure**: Declaring which port the service listens on helps documentation and tools like Docker Compose.

To build and run this microservice container:

```
# Build the image

docker build -t notifications-service:1.0 .


# Run the container

docker run -d -p 3000:3000 notifications-service:1.0
```

The microservice is now accessible on localhost:3000 on the host machine. In production, you might use container orchestration systems or cloud services to run multiple replicas behind a load balancer.

Docker Compose for Local Environments

When developing microservices locally, you may need several containers running concurrently—e.g., a database, a cache layer, and multiple microservices. **Docker Compose** allows you to define multi-container setups with a single YAML file. For instance:

```
version: '3'
services:
 notifications:
  build:
   context: .
   dockerfile: Dockerfile
  ports:
   - "3000:3000"
  environment:
   - NODE_ENV=development
   - REDIS_HOST=redis
  depends_on:
   - redis
```

```
redis:

  image: redis:6-alpine
```

In this setup, the **notifications** service depends on Redis, ensuring Redis starts first. The notifications service can reach it via the hostname `redis` on the default port 6379. Compose orchestrates everything locally—handy for testing and debugging on a developer's machine.

6.1.2 Kubernetes and Other Orchestration Platforms

While Docker containers excel at packaging microservices, large-scale mobile applications often need a robust platform to **orchestrate** container deployment, scaling, and lifecycle management. **Kubernetes**, originally developed by Google, is the de facto standard in container orchestration. Other platforms include **Apache Mesos**, **HashiCorp Nomad**, and vendor-specific solutions like **Amazon ECS**.

Kubernetes Fundamentals

Kubernetes manages containers in **Pods**, schedules them on **Nodes** (host machines), and monitors their health via **Controllers** (e.g., **Deployments**, **StatefulSets**). At a high level:

1. **Deployment**: Describes the desired number of pod replicas for a microservice, along with update strategies (rolling updates, etc.).
2. **Service**: Provides a stable network endpoint (ClusterIP, NodePort, or LoadBalancer) for pods, implementing load balancing and DNS-based service discovery.
3. **Ingress**: Manages external access to microservices (HTTP/HTTPS). Commonly used for routing traffic to different services by path or host name.

Example: Kubernetes Deployment and Service

Below is a sample YAML snippet for deploying the same **notifications** microservice in a Kubernetes cluster:

```
apiVersion: apps/v1

kind: Deployment

metadata:

  name: notifications-deployment

spec:
```

```yaml
  replicas: 3
  selector:
    matchLabels:
      app: notifications
  template:
    metadata:
      labels:
        app: notifications
    spec:
      containers:
      - name: notifications-container
        image: notifications-service:1.0
        ports:
        - containerPort: 3000
        env:
          - name: NODE_ENV
            value: "production"
          - name: REDIS_HOST
            value: "redis-service"
---
apiVersion: v1
kind: Service
metadata:
  name: notifications-service
spec:
  selector:
```

```
    app: notifications

  ports:

   - protocol: TCP

    port: 3000

    targetPort: 3000

  type: ClusterIP
```

What This Does:

- **Deployment**: Creates three replicas (pods) of the notifications microservice for high availability and load balancing.
- **Service**: Exposes these pods internally at port 3000 under the name `notifications-service`. Other pods can connect to `notifications-service:3000` to access it.

Auto-Scaling for Mobile Traffic

A hallmark of Kubernetes is the **Horizontal Pod Autoscaler (HPA),** which scales the number of pod replicas based on CPU or custom metrics. For mobile apps that may receive bursty traffic (e.g., push notifications for a marketing campaign), auto-scaling is critical:

```
apiVersion: autoscaling/v2

kind: HorizontalPodAutoscaler

metadata:

  name: notifications-hpa

spec:

  scaleTargetRef:

    apiVersion: apps/v1

    kind: Deployment

    name: notifications-deployment

  minReplicas: 3
```

```
maxReplicas: 10

metrics:

 - type: Resource

   resource:

    name: cpu

    target:

      type: Utilization

      averageUtilization: 70
```

Here, if average CPU usage for the pods exceeds 70%, Kubernetes automatically increases the replica count—up to 10—to handle load. Similarly, if load decreases, Kubernetes scales back down to save resources.

Other Orchestration Platforms

- **Amazon ECS (Elastic Container Service)**: A fully managed container orchestration service deeply integrated with AWS.
- **HashiCorp Nomad**: A lightweight orchestrator that can manage containers and non-container workloads.
- **Azure Container Instances (ACI) + Azure Kubernetes Service (AKS)**: Microsoft's orchestrated container offerings.

Though each has unique features, the core concept remains the same: schedule containers across a cluster, maintain availability, and provide networking and resource management.

Diagram: High-Level Kubernetes Architecture

This structure shows how external traffic enters the cluster via an Ingress, then is routed to the correct Service, which forwards requests to one or more pods. The Deployment ensures the correct number of pod replicas are running at all times.

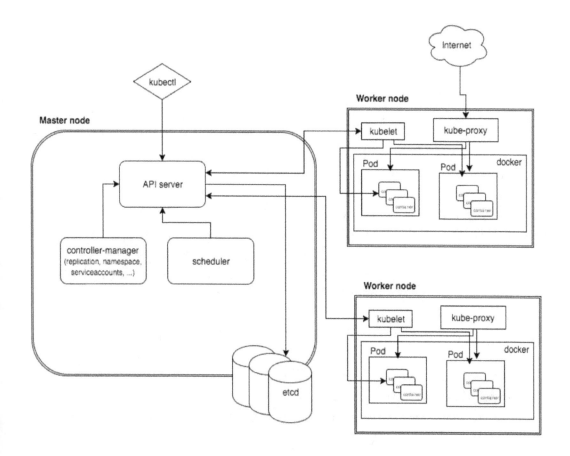

6.2 Serverless Microservices for Mobile

6.2.1 Pros and Cons of FaaS (Functions as a Service)

An alternative to container-based microservices is **Serverless** computing, often implemented via Functions as a Service (FaaS) offerings such as **AWS Lambda**, **Google Cloud Functions**, or **Azure Functions**. In this model, you write code as discrete functions that automatically scale with usage and are billed only for execution time.

Advantages:

1. **Pay-Per-Use**: You're only charged while your code runs, which may be cost-effective for sporadic or bursty workloads—common in mobile apps that see usage spikes around certain features or times.
2. **No Infrastructure Management**: The cloud provider handles provisioning, patching, and scaling.
3. **Rapid Development**: Teams can focus on writing code for specific tasks or endpoints rather than configuring servers.

Disadvantages:

1. **Cold Starts**: If a function isn't invoked for a while, the first call experiences a "cold start" overhead, which can degrade user experience in latency-sensitive mobile features.
2. **Limited Execution Time**: Many FaaS platforms impose timeouts (e.g., AWS Lambda's 15-minute limit). Long-running tasks may need other approaches or asynchronous splitting.
3. **Complex Orchestration**: Coordinating multiple functions (for multi-step workflows) can become complex, requiring additional logic or services like AWS Step Functions.

For **mobile microservices**, serverless can be attractive for tasks like sending notifications, image processing, or data analytics that happen sporadically or in background workflows. However, functions that handle real-time user interactions may require strategies to mitigate cold starts (e.g., warming functions periodically or using a specialized runtime) or might be better served by a container-based approach.

6.2.2 Integrating Serverless Components with Containerized Services

Modern architectures often blend serverless functions with containerized microservices. For instance, your **core** high-traffic services (e.g., authentication, feed generation) may run on Kubernetes for consistent performance, while event-driven tasks (e.g., processing user-uploaded images or logs) are offloaded to Lambda.

Possible Integration Points:

1. **Event-Driven Workflows**: A container-based service publishes an event to a queue (like Amazon SQS or Google Pub/Sub). A serverless function subscribes and processes these events asynchronously.
2. **API Gateway Routing**: A single API Gateway can route some endpoints to containerized microservices and others to serverless functions.
3. **Background Tasks**: If a microservice detects a large or CPU-heavy operation, it can invoke a serverless function asynchronously to handle it, freeing the microservice to respond quickly to the mobile user.

Example: Hybrid Architecture Diagram

This setup leverages the strengths of both containerized microservices (predictable, lower-latency operations that can scale horizontally) and serverless (cost-effectiveness and easy concurrency for sporadic or CPU-intensive tasks).

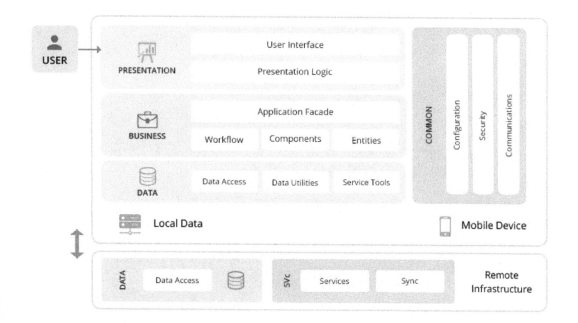

6.3 CI/CD Pipelines

6.3.1 Automating Builds and Tests for Each Service

A core tenet of microservices is the autonomy to **build and release** independently. **Continuous Integration (CI)** ensures every code commit triggers automated builds and tests, catching issues early. **Continuous Delivery/Deployment (CD)** extends this by making new versions of each microservice deployable—or actually deploying them—on every successful test run.

The CI/CD Pipeline Lifecycle

1. **Code Commit**: A developer pushes changes to a version-control repository (Git).
2. **Automated Build**: A CI system (like Jenkins, GitLab CI, GitHub Actions, or CircleCI) compiles the code, runs tests, and, if successful, builds a Docker image.
3. **Automated Testing**: Unit tests, integration tests, static analysis, and possibly performance checks are executed. For mobile microservices, you might also run specialized tests simulating mobile traffic patterns.
4. **Image Tagging and Registry**: If tests pass, the Docker image is tagged (e.g., v1. 2. 3) and pushed to a container registry (like Docker Hub, Amazon ECR, or Google Container Registry).
5. **Deploy or Stage**: The new image is deployed to a staging environment for further validation. Once approved, the pipeline can automatically or manually promote the image to production.

Example: Jenkinsfile Snippet for CI

```
pipeline {
  agent any

  stages {
    stage('Checkout') {
      steps {
        checkout scm
      }
    }
    stage('Build') {
      steps {
        sh 'docker build -t myorg/notifications-service:${BUILD_NUMBER} .'
      }
    }
    stage('Test') {
      steps {
        sh 'docker run --rm myorg/notifications-service:${BUILD_NUMBER} npm test'
      }
    }
    stage('Push Image') {
      steps {
        withCredentials([string(credentialsId: 'docker-registry-token', variable: 'TOKEN')]) {
          sh "echo $TOKEN | docker login -u myorg --password-stdin"
          sh "docker push myorg/notifications-service:${BUILD_NUMBER}"
        }
      }
```

```
        }

    }

}
```

How It Works:

- **Build**: Jenkins checks out the code, builds a Docker image, and tags it with `${BUILD_NUMBER}`.
- **Test**: The pipeline runs the container to execute tests.
- **Push Image**: After successful tests, the pipeline logs in to the Docker registry and pushes the new image.

6.3.2 Continuous Deployment Workflows

Continuous Deployment (CD) goes further by automatically rolling out changes to production if certain conditions are met (e.g., tests pass, a canary deployment has acceptable error rates). Key strategies include:

1. **Blue-Green Deployments**: Maintain two identical production environments, "blue" and "green." When deploying a new version, traffic is switched to the new environment only when it's fully ready. If issues arise, you can instantly revert to the old environment.
2. **Rolling Updates**: Kubernetes Deployments can roll out new versions of pods gradually. If the new version fails liveness checks or causes high error rates, the rollout halts or rolls back automatically.
3. **Canary Releases**: Route a small percentage of traffic to the new version initially (e.g., 5%). If performance and error metrics remain within acceptable thresholds, gradually increase the percentage. Otherwise, revert to the previous version.

Canary Release Example with Kubernetes

```
apiVersion: networking.k8s.io/v1

kind: Ingress

metadata:

  name: notifications-ingress

spec:
```

```
rules:
  - host: notifications.example.com
    http:
      paths:
      - path: /
        pathType: Prefix
        backend:
          service:
            name: notifications-service-stable
            port:
              number: 3000
      - path: /canary
        pathType: Prefix
        backend:
          service:
            name: notifications-service-canary
            port:
              number: 3000
```

You might route most users to notifications-service-stable while a small subset hitting /canary path is routed to notifications-service-canary. Over time, you can shift more traffic if metrics look good.

Mobile-Specific Considerations: Frequent app updates can lead to a wide range of client versions in the wild. Automated canary deployments let you test new backend endpoints or API changes in production with minimal user impact, ensuring older clients remain functional while gradually rolling out new features.

6.4 Multi-Cloud and Hybrid Deployments

6.4.1 Avoiding Vendor Lock-In

Mobile applications with global reach often use **multi-cloud** or **hybrid** strategies for resilience and coverage. Placing services in multiple providers (AWS, Azure, GCP) or mixing on-premises data centers with cloud environments can help:

- **Redundancy**: If one cloud region suffers an outage, traffic can fail over to another region or provider.
- **Performance**: Route users to the geographically closest data center or provider for lower latency.
- **Regulatory Requirements**: Some industries or regions require data to stay within specific jurisdictions.

Challenges:

- **Different APIs and Tools**: Each cloud has unique offerings. Minimizing reliance on proprietary features (e.g., a managed database that only exists in one cloud) can reduce lock-in.
- **Networking Complexity**: Setting up VPNs or direct connections between providers is non-trivial and can affect security and cost.

Infrastructure-as-Code

To keep multi-cloud setups manageable, teams often use **Infrastructure-as-Code (IaC)** tools like **Terraform**, **Pulumi**, or **Crossplane**. An example Terraform snippet for creating a Kubernetes cluster on AWS might look like this:

```
provider "aws" {
  region = "us-east-1"
}


resource "aws_eks_cluster" "my_cluster" {
  name    = "my-eks-cluster"
  role_arn = aws_iam_role.eks_role.arn


  vpc_config {
    subnet_ids = [aws_subnet.subnet1.id, aws_subnet.subnet2.id]

  }
```

```
}
```

You could then replicate a similar definition in another region or cloud, ensuring consistent infrastructure provisioning across environments. This fosters a multi-cloud approach without manually configuring each platform.

6.4.2 Managing Cross-Cloud Traffic and Security

When microservices span different clouds or hybrid environments, secure and efficient communication is paramount.

1. **Inter-Service Connectivity**: Use **encrypted tunnels** (e.g., TLS or VPNs) or **service meshes** (e.g., Istio, Linkerd) that unify security policies across clusters.
2. **Global Load Balancing**: Solutions like **Cloudflare**, **AWS Route 53 Traffic Flow**, or **GCP Load Balancing** can direct users to the nearest or healthiest region.
3. **Observability**: Ensure logs, metrics, and traces flow into a unified system (e.g., a centralized ELK stack or a multi-cloud SaaS monitoring tool). Cross-cloud debugging can be painful if each region has siloed telemetry.

Example: Diagram of a Multi-Cloud Deployment

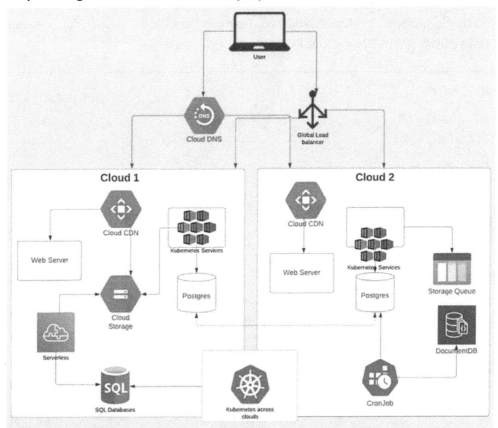

A mobile app can connect globally, with traffic directed to the nearest region. Inter-cloud traffic between AWS EKS and GCP GKE might be encrypted with mutual TLS or a secure VPN. On-prem resources are also connected for legacy databases or specialized hardware needs.

Extended Considerations for Mobile Microservices

While the above sections focus on the core building blocks of deployment and infrastructure, certain **mobile-centric** aspects warrant special attention:

1. **API Gateway or Edge Services**: As discussed in Chapter 4's communication patterns, a single gateway can route traffic to multiple microservices. Choose a globally distributed or multi-region gateway if your mobile user base is spread worldwide.
2. **Autoscaling Policies**: Mobile usage patterns can be unpredictable—users might spike in one region at a specific local time. Resource auto-scaling must be configured with metrics tailored to your domain (e.g., requests per second, concurrency, CPU, or custom app metrics).
3. **Deployment Frequency**: Rapid iteration for bug fixes or new features is common in mobile. Ensure your pipeline supports quick rollbacks or hotfix deployments, especially if you discover a regression or critical bug after pushing a new version.
4. **Rollback and Versioning**: Legacy mobile clients might rely on older API endpoints. Maintain backward-compatible routes or keep older container versions available until you're certain client usage has shifted to newer releases.

Chapter 7: Observability and Monitoring

Modern microservice architectures often involve dozens (or even hundreds) of services, each with its own codebase, database, and deployment pipeline. For **mobile-focused** systems, this complexity is magnified by unpredictable traffic patterns, frequent feature rollouts to keep pace with app store releases, and user expectations for responsive, always-available experiences.

7.1 Logging and Aggregation

7.1.1 Why Logging Matters for Microservices

In any software system, logs provide a historical record of what has happened. In a **microservices** architecture, these logs become far more crucial—and complex—to manage:

- **Distributed Environment**: A single user request can involve multiple microservices, each producing its own logs in separate containers or nodes.
- **Temporary Instances**: Container orchestration platforms (like Kubernetes) can spin up or tear down microservice replicas dynamically, so logs must be centralized before the containers vanish.
- **Varying Log Formats**: Different languages, frameworks, and logging libraries can generate disparate log outputs, complicating correlation and analysis.

With robust **logging and aggregation**, teams can efficiently:

- Debug user-facing errors by tracing requests across services.
- Identify trends or anomalies (e.g., repeated errors for a specific feature).

- Audit critical actions (like financial transactions) for compliance or security.

7.1.2 Structured Logging Best Practices

Structured logs store data in a well-defined format (e.g., JSON) rather than relying on free-form text. This approach enables:

1. **Machine-Readable**: Tools like Elasticsearch, Splunk, or Loki can parse JSON logs for faster search and analytics.
2. **Consistent Fields**: Each log entry might include fields such as `timestamp`, `serviceName`, `requestId`, `severity`, and `message`, making it straightforward to filter by specific criteria.
3. **Correlation**: By including a `traceId` or `spanId` in every log, you can link logs to distributed traces, bridging the gap between textual logs and request-level instrumentation (discussed further in Section 7.3).

Example: Node.js Logging with Winston

Below is a code snippet showing how to produce structured JSON logs using the **Winston** library in a Node.js microservice (e.g., "PushNotificationService"):

```
// logger.js
const { createLogger, format, transports } = require('winston');


const logger = createLogger({
  level: 'info',
  format: format.json(),
  defaultMeta: { service: 'push-notification-service' },
  transports: [
    new transports.Console()
  ]
});


module.exports = logger;
```

```
// usage in a service file

const logger = require('./logger');


function sendPushNotification(userId, message) {
  logger.info({
    event: 'SendPushNotification',
    userId,
    message
  });


  // Actual push notification logic...
  // ...
}


module.exports = { sendPushNotification };
```

Key Points:

- `format.json()` ensures logs are emitted as JSON objects rather than unstructured strings.
- Each log entry includes a consistent set of fields like `service: 'push-notification-service'`.
- Additional metadata—such as `userId` and `event`—makes it simpler to filter or query logs in a centralized system.

7.1.3 Centralized Log Aggregation

When running dozens of microservice instances across multiple servers or containers, shipping logs to a centralized system is essential. Common approaches include:

1. **Logging Agents (Filebeat, Fluent Bit, Vector)**: Lightweight daemons that run on each host or container, reading log files (or standard output) and forwarding them to a log aggregator.
2. **Direct Library Integration**: Some logging libraries can send logs directly to services like Elasticsearch or Splunk, though this can become cumbersome to manage.
3. **Sidecar Containers**: In Kubernetes, you can deploy a sidecar container that collects logs from the main microservice container and ships them to a remote aggregator.

Popular Log Aggregation Tools

- **Elasticsearch/Logstash/Kibana (ELK Stack)**: A popular open-source solution that ingests logs into Elasticsearch and uses Kibana for dashboards.
- **Grafana Loki**: A more recent solution that focuses on storing and querying logs efficiently, integrating closely with Grafana.
- **Splunk**: A commercial platform that offers powerful search, machine learning, and correlation features for enterprise-scale logs.

Diagram: Log Flow in a Containerized Environment

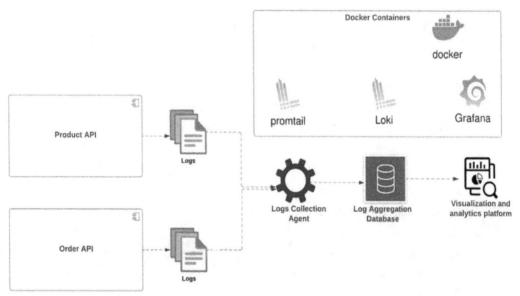

7.1.4 Near Real-Time Analysis of Logs

Real-time log analysis can be pivotal when debugging mobile-specific spikes, such as a new version of the mobile app causing thousands of errors after an update:

- **Alerting on Log Patterns**: Tools like Kibana can watch for patterns—e.g., a specific error message spiking above 100 occurrences per minute.

- **Dashboards**: Visualize the volume of logs by severity or service. For instance, seeing error logs spike for the "PaymentsService" after a promotional campaign can reveal capacity or code issues.

In production, you'll likely combine logs with **metrics** (Section 7.2) and **traces** (Section 7.3) to form a full picture. Logs alone can be noisy, especially if you rely heavily on them for ephemeral debugging data. Consider using logs primarily for post-incident forensics and near real-time pattern matching, while letting metrics and tracing handle system health and request-level analysis.

7.2 Metrics and Instrumentation

7.2.1 Key Metrics for Mobile-Focused Microservices

Metrics are numerical representations of system behavior, tracked at regular intervals. While logs capture discrete events, **metrics** reveal trends: CPU usage, request latency, error rates, queue lengths, etc. For mobile microservices, some specific metrics include:

1. **Request Rate (RPS)**: Requests per second to a particular microservice. Mobile traffic can spike around app feature promotions or time-specific usage patterns (e.g., lunch time for a food-delivery app).
2. **Latency (p95, p99)**: The 95th or 99th percentile of request duration. Mobile apps can be sensitive to latency, especially on cellular networks.
3. **Error Rate**: Proportion of requests returning 4xx or 5xx responses. May spike after a new client release.
4. **Push Notification Delivery**: For a push-notification microservice, track how many notifications are successfully enqueued and delivered.
5. **Database Query Performance**: Slow queries may cause cascading delays across services.
6. **Cache Hit Ratio**: If you cache results for mobile clients, monitor the ratio of hits to misses to gauge caching effectiveness.

7.2.2 OpenTelemetry for Instrumentation

OpenTelemetry is an emerging standard for instrumenting, generating, and exporting telemetry data (logs, metrics, traces) across different languages and platforms. It supports a unified approach:

- **Language-Specific SDKs**: For Node.js, Java, Python, Go, etc.
- **Auto-Instrumentation**: Many frameworks (Express, Spring Boot) can automatically capture metrics like request counts and latencies without manual code changes.

- **Exporters**: Send data to your choice of backends, such as Prometheus, Jaeger, or Zipkin.

Example: Instrumenting a Node.js Service with OpenTelemetry

Below is a simplified snippet that demonstrates capturing HTTP request metrics:

```javascript
// instrumentation.js
const { MeterProvider } = require('@opentelemetry/metrics');
const { PrometheusExporter } = require('@opentelemetry/exporter-prometheus');


const meterProvider = new MeterProvider();
const exporter = new PrometheusExporter({ startServer: true });


meterProvider.addExporter(exporter);
const meter = meterProvider.getMeter('mobile-metrics');


const requestCount = meter.createCounter('http_request_count', {
  description: 'Counts all incoming HTTP requests',
});


function recordRequest(req, res, next) {
  requestCount.add(1, { route: req.path, method: req.method });
  next();
}


module.exports = recordRequest;
```

In your main service file:

```
const express = require('express');

const recordRequest = require('./instrumentation');

const app = express();


app.use(recordRequest); // captures request metrics


app.get('/hello', (req, res) => {

  res.send('Hello World!');

});


app.listen(3000, () => {

  console.log('Service running on port 3000');

});
```

Key Points:

- A **Prometheus Exporter** is started on a default port (often :9464), exposing metrics in the format Prometheus expects.
- The code increments a counter for each incoming request, labeling by route and method.
- Tools like Prometheus or Grafana can scrape these metrics to create dashboards or trigger alerts.

7.2.3 Prometheus and Grafana for Metrics Collection and Visualization

Prometheus is a popular open-source system for collecting and storing metrics, especially well-integrated with Kubernetes. It "scrapes" metrics endpoints (like the OpenTelemetry Prometheus exporter) at intervals. Key features:

- **Dimensional Data Model**: Each metric can include labels (e.g., service, method, status_code) to slice and dice data in queries.
- **Powerful Query Language (PromQL)**: Allows for complex aggregations, like rate(http_request_count[1m]) to measure requests per second.

- **Alertmanager Integration**: You can define alerting rules—e.g., if 5xx error rates exceed 5% for more than 2 minutes, send an alert.

Grafana is typically paired with Prometheus to visualize metrics in dashboards. You can create custom panels showing:

- **Request Rate Over Time**
- **Latency Histograms**
- **Error Rate Stacked by Service**
- **Database Query Performance**
- **Custom Mobile KPIs** (like push notification success rates or offline sync failures)

Diagram: Metrics Flow with Prometheus

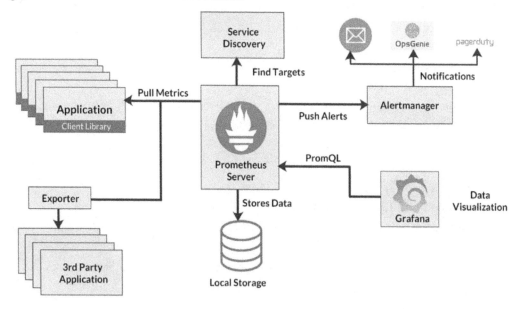

7.2.4 Advanced Metrics Techniques

- **Histograms**: Track the distribution of request latencies or payload sizes. Allows you to generate p95 or p99 percentile data.
- **Push vs. Pull**: Prometheus primarily "pulls" metrics. In some scenarios, you might use a "pushgateway" if a service is short-lived and can't be scraped.
- **High-Cardinality Labels**: Be wary of labeling metrics with user IDs or session IDs, as this can explode your metric storage. Focus on aggregated labels (e.g., region, endpoint, status_code) for more sustainable usage.

7.3 Distributed Tracing

7.3.1 Why Distributed Tracing is Vital

In a microservices environment, a single user request can traverse multiple services—**UserService → AuthService → ProductService → BillingService**, and so on. When a request fails or becomes slow, logs and metrics may hint at a problem, but **distributed tracing** allows you to see the exact path, including how much time was spent in each service or database call.

For **mobile apps**, distributed tracing is particularly valuable because:

- The user may experience slow responses if just one microservice in the chain is lagging.
- Mobile connectivity can be volatile, so determining whether latency originates in the backend or the client is key.
- Identifying which specific microservice or endpoint is causing bottlenecks reduces guesswork in large infrastructures.

7.3.2 Fundamentals of Spans and Traces

A **trace** represents an entire request's journey. It consists of **spans**, each representing a specific operation within a service—e.g., "AuthService: ValidateToken()" or "ProductService: Query Database." Spans have:

- **Name**: e.g., `/GET /api/v1/products`
- **Start and End Timestamps**: Used to calculate duration.
- **Context**: A unique trace ID and a span ID. The parent span ID is the operation that triggered the current one.
- **Metadata**: Optional tags and logs that store additional details (like an error code, the user ID, or the item ID in a product lookup).

7.3.3 Implementing Tracing Tools (Jaeger, Zipkin, OpenTelemetry)

Multiple tracing backends exist:

- **Zipkin**: One of the earliest distributed tracing systems, focusing on simplicity.
- **Jaeger**: An open-source solution created by Uber, offering advanced features like adaptive sampling and an intuitive UI.
- **OpenTelemetry**: A standard that can export trace data to Jaeger, Zipkin, or other backends.

Example: Using OpenTelemetry with Jaeger

Below is a Node.js snippet demonstrating how to set up an OpenTelemetry **Tracer** that exports to Jaeger:

```
// tracer.js

const { NodeTracerProvider } = require('@opentelemetry/sdk-trace-node');

const { BatchSpanProcessor } = require('@opentelemetry/sdk-trace-base');

const { JaegerExporter } = require('@opentelemetry/exporter-jaeger');

const { ExpressInstrumentation } = require('@opentelemetry/instrumentation-express');


const provider = new NodeTracerProvider();


// Configure Jaeger exporter
const exporter = new JaegerExporter({
  endpoint: 'http://jaeger-collector:14268/api/traces'
});
provider.addSpanProcessor(new BatchSpanProcessor(exporter));


// Auto-instrument Express routes
const instrumentation = new ExpressInstrumentation();
instrumentation.setTracerProvider(provider);


provider.register();


module.exports = provider.getTracer('mobile-tracer');
```

In your Express application:

```
const express = require('express');
const tracer = require('./tracer'); // ensures the tracer is initialized
const app = express();
```

```
app.get('/profile', (req, res) => {

  // The instrumentation library automatically creates spans for /profile

  res.json({ user: 'Alice', points: 120 });

});



app.listen(3000, () => console.log('Tracing example running on port 3000'));
```

What Happens:

- The **ExpressInstrumentation** intercepts each incoming request, creating a span with a name like `GET /profile`.
- The library automatically propagates trace context across local function calls, and you can also configure it to propagate context to downstream HTTP calls.
- Spans are batched and sent to Jaeger, which you can then visualize in the Jaeger UI, seeing each request's timeline across services.

7.3.4 Visualizing Traces and Identifying Bottlenecks

In a tool like **Jaeger**, each trace appears as a **gantt-like chart**. You might see:

1. **Root Span**: "GET /profile" in the API Gateway.
2. **Child Span**: "UserService: DB Query" taking 15ms.
3. **Another Child Span**: "AnalyticsService: CreateUserStats" taking 200ms.
4. **PushNotificationService**: Possibly triggered if the user earned a new badge, etc.

If a request is slow, you can spot which microservice or database call dominates the timeline. Suppose "AnalyticsService" shows a 150ms jump after a recent update; you can zero in on that code rather than rummaging through logs across multiple microservices.

7.3.5 Sampling and Overhead

Tracing every request can be expensive at high traffic volumes. Many systems implement **sampling**—only tracing, say, 1% or a fixed number of requests. Even this partial data can yield valuable insights, though critical or error-prone paths might be traced at a higher rate. Tools like Jaeger can use **adaptive sampling**, dynamically adjusting the sampling rate based on error rates or service load to capture more data when issues arise.

7.4 Alerting and Incident Response

7.4.1 Automated Alert Mechanisms

Even with comprehensive logs, metrics, and tracing, your observability platform should automatically **alert** relevant teams when anomalies occur. For mobile microservices, you might define alerts around:

- **High 5xx Error Rates**: If error rates exceed 2% on the "PaymentService" for more than 1 minute, you likely have an incident.
- **Increased Latency**: p95 latency spiking above 500ms for certain critical endpoints (like "Login" or "Checkout").
- **Resource Exhaustion**: CPU usage on a cluster node hitting 90%, memory usage consistently above thresholds, or the number of container restarts spiking.

Tools like **Prometheus Alertmanager**, **PagerDuty**, or **Opsgenie** can route these alerts to on-call staff via SMS, phone calls, or Slack channels. Setting **proper thresholds** and **alert severity** is crucial to avoid false positives that create alert fatigue.

7.4.2 On-Call Rotations

In many organizations, microservice-based architectures demand multiple teams, each responsible for specific domains (e.g., "Billing," "Notifications," "Analytics"). Setting up on-call rotations ensures that:

1. **24/7 Coverage**: Mobile traffic is global, so issues can arise at any hour.
2. **Subject Matter Expertise**: Incidents in "BillingService" page the correct team, who knows the code and can fix the issue rapidly.
3. **Escalation Policies**: If the first on-call engineer doesn't acknowledge within a set time, the alert escalates to a second on-call or a manager.

7.4.3 Service-Level Objectives (SLOs)

Service-Level Objectives define target reliability or performance metrics. For instance, "The Notification Service must respond to 99.5% of push requests within 200ms." Observability tools measure the actual performance (SLI, or Service-Level Indicator) and compare it against the target SLO. If an SLO is consistently not met, the team must undertake reliability improvements or re-architect certain components.

Example SLO Statement

SLO: 99% of requests to `POST` `/api/v1/push` succeed with a response time under 300ms over a 30-day window. **SLI**: Derived from Prometheus metrics, e.g., `histogram_quantile(0.99,` `sum(rate(http_request_duration_seconds_bucket{endpoint="/api/v1/p` `ush"}[5m])) by (le))`.

By connecting these metrics to your alerting system, you can raise early warnings when the error budget (the allowed portion of unavailability or slow performance) is nearing exhaustion.

7.4.4 Incident Triage and Runbooks

When an alert fires, teams perform **incident triage**:

1. **Identify the Impact**: Which microservice is failing or degraded? Are mobile users receiving errors?
2. **Consult Runbooks**: A runbook is a documented procedure for diagnosing and fixing common issues. For example, "If the NotificationService CPU usage is 100% and queue length is high, scale out the deployment or flush old messages from the queue."
3. **Collaborate**: For multi-service breakdowns, a cross-team Slack or incident call might be formed. Observability data is shared so each service's logs, metrics, and traces can be collectively examined.
4. **Postmortem**: After the incident, a blameless postmortem identifies root causes (e.g., a memory leak in a recent deployment) and improvements to monitoring (like adding new metrics for memory usage thresholds).

7.5 Special Considerations for Mobile Applications

Though the focus in this chapter is on **server-side** observability, mobile apps often feed critical data back to your microservices environment. Some additional angles:

1. **Client Metrics & Crash Reporting**: Tools like Firebase Crashlytics, Sentry, or Bugsnag gather client-side errors or performance data. Teams correlate them with server logs to see if a spike in client crashes aligns with certain API errors.
2. **Real User Monitoring (RUM)**: Captures network request times from the actual mobile device's perspective. Differences between server-side latency and client-side perceived latency might reveal issues like poor connectivity or large payloads.
3. **Push Delivery Analytics**: Especially for real-time features or notifications, track how many pushes were enqueued vs. how many the client acknowledges. This can highlight downstream issues with Apple Push Notification service (APNs) or Firebase Cloud Messaging (FCM).

4. **API Version Usage**: Mobile apps might remain on old versions. Observability systems can track usage by API version, ensuring older endpoints remain healthy until they can be deprecated or forcibly upgraded.

By integrating **client-side** data with **server-side** logs, metrics, and traces, you gain a complete view of user experience—pinpointing whether the cause of a slowdown is an under-provisioned microservice, a suboptimal caching layer, or the user's cellular network.

7.6 Putting It All Together: A Real-World Example

Imagine a scenario:

- A new version of the mobile app rolls out with a redesigned purchase flow. Suddenly, your **OrdersService** sees a 30% spike in error rates and a jump in 500ms+ latencies.
- Your metrics dashboard (Prometheus + Grafana) triggers an alert at 11 PM local time, notifying the on-call engineer that **p95 latency** is above the threshold and error rates are climbing.
- The on-call engineer checks distributed tracing in Jaeger to see that the "PaymentService -> ThirdPartyPaymentAPI" call accounts for most of the slowdown. Perhaps the new flow is adding extra validation steps, or the external payment API is hitting rate limits.
- Logs from the "PaymentService" (aggregated in Elasticsearch) confirm the external API is returning `429 Too Many Requests` occasionally.
- The engineer references a runbook for "PaymentService external API rate-limit incidents." They find instructions to reduce concurrency or contact the payment provider.
- Meanwhile, the mobile dev team is alerted to see if the client is re-sending requests too quickly. Possibly the new UI triggers multiple payment attempts if the user taps twice.
- Once the immediate fix is applied (throttle the calls or raise the external API limit), the system recovers, and latencies return to normal. The on-call logs an incident postmortem to refine the SLO and add a new metric tracking the external API's `429` responses.

This chain of events underscores how **logs, metrics, traces, and alerting** converge to swiftly diagnose and resolve issues in a microservices environment, especially one supporting a mobile app with rapid changes and potentially high concurrency.

In conclusion, Observability and Monitoring highlights the critical role of robust telemetry in microservices architectures that power mobile applications. By implementing cohesive strategies across **logging, metrics, distributed tracing, and incident response**, engineering teams can drastically reduce **MTTR** (Mean Time to Repair) and maintain high availability despite the complexities of distributed systems and mobile traffic patterns.

Chapter 8: Security and Compliance

As mobile applications become more sophisticated, they often rely on intricate microservices architectures—deployed across distributed environments—to handle sensitive data such as user profiles, financial transactions, healthcare information, or personal communications. **Security** and **compliance** thus emerge as paramount concerns. A single data breach or misconfiguration can expose thousands (or millions) of user records, disrupt brand trust, and result in costly regulatory fines.

8.1 Authentication and Authorization in a Mobile Context

8.1.1 Token-Based Authentication (JWT, OAuth 2.0)

Mobile apps typically communicate with microservices over HTTP/HTTPS. One of the most widespread ways to authenticate and authorize these requests is through **token-based mechanisms** such as JSON Web Tokens (JWT) or OAuth 2.0 tokens.

JSON Web Tokens (JWT)

A **JWT** is a compact token—often consisting of a header, payload, and signature—used to assert claims about an authenticated user (or client). For mobile scenarios:

1. **Header**: Declares token type (JWT) and signing algorithm (e.g., HS256, RS256).
2. **Payload**: Contains claims such as sub (subject/user ID), iat (issued-at time), exp (expiration), and custom claims like roles.

3. **Signature**: Ensures integrity; microservices verify it with a shared secret (HMAC) or a public key (RSA/ECDSA).

A typical JWT might look like:

```
eyJhbGciOiJSUzI1NiIsInR5cCI6IkpXVCJ9.

eyJzdWIiOiIxMjM0NTYiLCJuYW1lIjoiQWxpY2UiLCJyb2xlcyI6WyJVU0VSIiwiQURNSU4iXSwia
WF0IjoxNjg2MTIzNDM4LCJleHAiOjE2ODYxMjcwMzh9.

[signature]
```

Mobile applications usually obtain this token upon successful login and include it in the Authorization header for subsequent requests:

```
Authorization: Bearer <JWT_token_here>
```

On the server side, each microservice verifies the token's signature, checks expiration, and ensures roles or permissions match the requested resource. Libraries in various languages (Node.js, Java, Python) provide straightforward ways to decode and validate JWTs.

Code Example: Node.js JWT Validation

```javascript
const jwt = require('jsonwebtoken');


function verifyJWT(req, res, next) {
  const authHeader = req.headers.authorization;
  if (!authHeader) {
   return res.status(401).json({ error: 'Missing Authorization header' });
  }


  const token = authHeader.split(' ')[1];
  try {
   const decoded = jwt.verify(token, process.env.JWT_PUBLIC_KEY, { algorithms: ['RS256'] });
```

```
  req.user = decoded; // Attach user info to the request object

  next();

} catch (err) {

  return res.status(403).json({ error: 'Invalid token' });

}

}


module.exports = verifyJWT;
```

Key Mobile Considerations:

- **Token Storage**: On mobile, store tokens securely (e.g., in iOS Keychain or Android Keystore). Avoid insecure local storage that can be accessed by malicious apps.
- **Token Expiration**: Use short-lived tokens (e.g., 15 minutes to 1 hour) to reduce risk if a token is stolen. A refresh token flow ensures the app can quietly obtain a new token without forcing the user to re-login frequently.

OAuth 2.0

OAuth 2.0 is a broader framework for delegated authorization. Mobile apps can use flows like **Authorization Code with PKCE** (Proof Key for Code Exchange) to securely exchange an authorization code for tokens without exposing client secrets. This is especially relevant for apps that integrate with third-party services or require single sign-on across multiple microservices.

PKCE Flow (high-level steps):

1. The mobile app generates a **code verifier** (random string) and a **code challenge** (hashed version of the verifier).
2. It redirects the user to the OAuth authorization server with the code challenge.
3. After user login, the authorization server returns an authorization code.
4. The app exchanges the code plus the original **code verifier** for an access token.
5. If the code challenge and verifier match, the server issues the token. This mitigates interception attacks since the code can't be used without the correct verifier.

Diagram: OAuth 2.0 PKCE Flow for Mobile

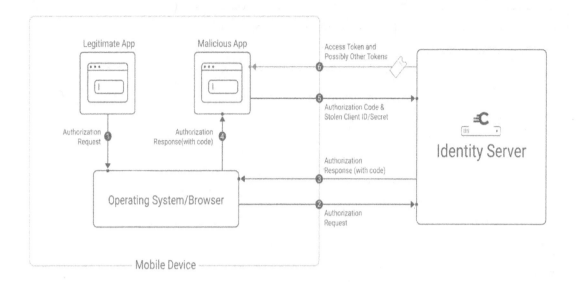

Mobile Device

Benefits for microservices:

- **Centralized Authentication**: Each microservice trusts the OAuth server, validating tokens from the same issuer.
- **Delegated Permissions**: The token's scope or claims determine which microservice endpoints the user can access.

8.1.2 Integrating Mobile Clients with Single Sign-On (SSO)

Single Sign-On (SSO) allows users to authenticate once and gain access to multiple microservices without repeated logins—valuable in multi-feature mobile apps (e.g., a super-app with ridesharing, food delivery, and payments). Common SSO protocols include **SAML** and **OpenID Connect (OIDC)**. While SAML is more enterprise-oriented, OIDC is built on top of OAuth 2.0 for web and mobile use cases.

OIDC extends OAuth 2.0 with an ID token (JWT) that carries user identity claims like name, email, and picture. The mobile app can store and present this ID token to microservices that trust the same identity provider (IdP).

Example: Microservice Checking OIDC ID Token

```
import jwt

import requests


OIDC_ISSUER = "https://accounts.example.com"
```

```
OIDC_JWKS_URL = "https://accounts.example.com/.well-known/jwks.json"


# One-time fetch of JWKS for signature verification

jwks = requests.get(OIDC_JWKS_URL).json()


def verify_oidc_id_token(token):
    # decode header to find key ID (kid)

    unverified_header = jwt.get_unverified_header(token)

    kid = unverified_header.get("kid")


    # find matching public key in JWKS

    for key in jwks["keys"]:

        if key["kid"] == kid:

            public_key = # build RSA public key from key["n"], key["e"]

            break


    # verify signature and issuer

    payload = jwt.decode(token, public_key, algorithms=["RS256"], audience="my-mobile-
app", issuer=OIDC_ISSUER)

    return payload
```

In practice, libraries or frameworks handle the complexity of fetching JSON Web Key Sets (JWKS) and verifying OIDC tokens. The principle remains the same: each microservice ensures the token is valid, not expired, and was issued by the trusted IdP.

8.1.3 Handling Offline or Low-Connectivity Scenarios

Mobile users often experience spotty network coverage, complicating authentication flows. Some strategies:

- **Caching Tokens**: The app may keep an **access token** (and refresh token) so it can function for a short period offline, then refresh once online.
- **Grace Period**: If a token is close to expiring but the user is offline, certain microservices might allow minimal usage until connectivity is restored, balancing security with user experience.
- **Device-based Biometrics**: Some organizations implement local device authentication (Touch ID, Face ID) to let users access partial offline data. True server-side actions still require a valid token once connectivity returns.

8.2 Securing Service-to-Service Communication

While user-to-service security is crucial, many attacks target **internal traffic** between microservices. If an attacker gains a foothold in one service, they might pivot to others unless strong controls are in place.

8.2.1 Mutual TLS (mTLS) and Other Encryption Strategies

mTLS ensures both the client and server present certificates during the TLS handshake, verifying each other's identity. In a microservices architecture:

1. Each service is issued an X.509 certificate from a trusted internal certificate authority (CA).
2. When Service A connects to Service B, they perform a TLS handshake. B verifies A's certificate against the CA, and A verifies B's certificate similarly.
3. All traffic is encrypted, and only services with valid certs can communicate.

Advantages:

- **Zero Trust**: Even if the network is compromised, each request requires valid TLS certificates.
- **Granular Access Control**: You can configure policies that only certain services can call certain endpoints based on certificate attributes.

Drawbacks:

- **Certificate Management Overhead**: Automating certificate issuance and rotation is nontrivial. Tools like **HashiCorp Vault**, **cert-manager** (for Kubernetes), or a service mesh can streamline this process.

8.2.2 API Gateway or Service Mesh Security Policies

An **API gateway** can enforce a consistent security layer at the edge, requiring TLS, validating tokens, rate limiting, or rewriting headers. However, inside the network, microservices may still talk to each other directly. For deeper security, many teams adopt a **service mesh** (e.g., **Istio**, **Linkerd**, **Consul Connect**) that provides:

1. **Sidecar Proxies**: Each microservice instance runs a small proxy container that handles inbound/outbound traffic.
2. **mTLS by Default**: The mesh automates certificate issuance/renewal, ensuring every call is encrypted.
3. **Policy and Authorization**: The mesh can define rules like "Service Payment can only call Service Orders on port 8080 with a valid JWT."
4. **Observability**: Integrates metrics and tracing at the network layer.

Diagram: Service Mesh with mTLS

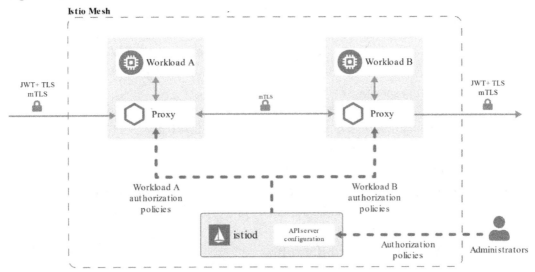

Each service instance has a sidecar. They trust the service mesh's CA to issue certificates. All traffic is encrypted at the sidecar level, removing the need to implement mTLS in each service's code.

8.2.3 API Gateway or Service Mesh Security Configurations: Example

Using **Istio** as an example, a simple YAML snippet that enforces mTLS might look like:

```
apiVersion: security.istio.io/v1beta1

kind: PeerAuthentication

metadata:

 name: default
```

```
spec:
  mtls:
    mode: STRICT
```

This config ensures all pods in the namespace require mutual TLS for inbound connections. Additional policies can specify which services or service accounts have permission to call each other, implementing a **zero-trust** model.

8.3 Protecting Data in Transit and at Rest

8.3.1 Encryption Standards for Sensitive Mobile Data

For data traveling between mobile clients and microservices, **HTTPS/TLS** is the baseline requirement. But certain features—like offline caching or background sync—may involve storing or transmitting sensitive data. Recommendations:

- **TLS 1.2 or Higher**: Avoid outdated protocols like SSL 3.0 or TLS 1.0/1.1.
- **HSTS (HTTP Strict Transport Security)**: Instructs clients to always use secure connections.
- **Certificate Pinning**: The mobile app can pin the server's certificate or public key, preventing man-in-the-middle attacks by untrusted certificate authorities.

8.3.2 Secrets Management and Vaults

Even if traffic is encrypted, you must handle secrets—like **database credentials**, **API keys**, **JWT signing keys**—securely. Hard-coding secrets in microservice code or environment variables is a major risk. Instead:

1. **HashiCorp Vault**: A popular tool that securely stores secrets, rotating credentials automatically. Microservices authenticate to Vault using methods like Kubernetes service accounts, then retrieve ephemeral credentials.
2. **AWS Secrets Manager / Azure Key Vault / GCP Secret Manager**: Cloud-native alternatives providing tight integration with each provider's IAM.

Example: Vault Integration

- **Approach**: A microservice runs in Kubernetes with a service account that has a Vault policy. On startup, it requests a temporary database password from Vault, which expires after a set time.

- **Benefit**: Even if an attacker exfiltrates the password, it quickly becomes invalid. Vault can also audit every secret request.

Code Snippet: Node.js with Vault

```
const vault = require('node-vault')({

  endpoint: 'http://vault:8200',

  token: process.env.VAULT_TOKEN

});


async function getDbCredentials() {

  const res = await vault.read('database/creds/my-db-role');

  const username = res.data.username;

  const password = res.data.password;

  return { username, password };

}
```

Note: This snippet assumes the microservice has an appropriate **VAULT_TOKEN** or uses some other Vault auth method. The credentials come from Vault, not from a config file or environment variable.

8.3.3 Encryption at Rest

Microservices often store user data in databases, object storage, or logs. Ensure **encryption at rest**:

- **Database-Level Encryption**: Many relational databases support **Transparent Data Encryption (TDE)** or table/column-level encryption.
- **File and Object Storage**: Tools like **AWS KMS** can encrypt S3 buckets or EBS volumes.
- **Key Management**: Track the lifecycle of encryption keys (creation, rotation, revocation). Typically, cloud KMS solutions or Vault handle this.

Mobile-Specific Consideration: Some data might be stored on the device (e.g., local user preferences, offline data). Use platform features like Android **EncryptedSharedPreferences** or iOS **Data Protection** classes (kSecAttrAccessibleWhenUnlocked, etc.) to ensure data is encrypted on disk. This is especially critical if your app caches PII, chat history, or financial data offline.

8.4 Regulatory and Compliance Considerations

Many mobile apps handle **personally identifiable information (PII)**, payment info, or health data. Failing to comply with relevant regulations can lead to legal repercussions and reputational harm.

8.4.1 GDPR, HIPAA, and Other Industry Regulations

1. **GDPR (General Data Protection Regulation)**: Applicable to EU residents' data. Key aspects:
   - **Data Subject Rights**: Deletion, rectification, portability, and the right to be forgotten.
   - **Consent and Transparency**: Users must know what data is collected and how it's processed.
   - **Data Protection by Design**: Security must be embedded from the outset.
2. **HIPAA (Health Insurance Portability and Accountability Act)**: For US healthcare data. Major requirements revolve around:
   - **Protected Health Information (PHI)**: Must be stored and transmitted securely, with logs of access.
   - **Business Associate Agreements (BAAs)** for any service handling PHI.
3. **PCI-DSS (Payment Card Industry Data Security Standard)**: For storing, transmitting, or processing cardholder data.
   - **Restricted Storage**: Never store full credit card numbers or CVV in logs.
   - **Network Segmentation**: Payment data often must be isolated from other system areas.
   - **Strong Access Control**: Unique IDs for each person with computer access, multi-factor authentication, etc.

Key Actions for microservices:

- **Data Minimization**: Only store what is strictly necessary.
- **Anonymization / Pseudonymization**: Convert real user data (e.g., name, address) into tokens or hashed IDs.
- **Breach Notification**: Have an incident response plan if a breach occurs (some regulations demand notification within 72 hours).
- **Consent Management**: For EU GDPR or similar laws, track user consent states in a central or easily queryable manner.

8.4.2 Implementing Audit Trails for Distributed Microservices

Regulators often require the ability to reconstruct events—who accessed or changed user data, when, and why. In a microservices architecture, data modifications might span multiple services and databases.

Approach:

1. **Centralized Audit Log**: Each service emits "audit events" (e.g., `{"type": "USER_DATA_CHANGE", "userId": "123", "changedBy": "adminUser", "timestamp": "2024-01-01T12:00:00Z"}`) to a secure, append-only system.
2. **Immutability**: Store logs in a **write-once** or **append-only** format. Solutions like **WORM (Write Once, Read Many)** storage or cryptographic signing of logs ensure tamper-evidence.
3. **Search and Export**: Provide tools or APIs that allow compliance officers to query logs for a specific user or timeframe.

Example: Python Microservice Emitting Audit Events

```python
import json

import requests

import datetime


def update_user_profile(user_id, new_data, actor):
    # update logic ...
    # after success, emit audit event
    event = {
        "type": "USER_DATA_CHANGE",
        "userId": user_id,
        "changedBy": actor,
        "timestamp": datetime.datetime.utcnow().isoformat() + "Z",
        "details": new_data
    }
    # POST to an internal "Audit Service" or message queue
    requests.post("http://audit-service:4000/audit-events", json=event)
```

Audit Service might store these events in a secure database or forward them to an external logging system that's tamper-resistant.

8.4.3 Data Retention, Deletion, and Subject Requests

For GDPR compliance or good data hygiene:

- **Retention Policies**: Define how long you store user data—e.g., 2 years for logs, 7 years for financial records.
- **Automated Deletion**: The system triggers deletion or anonymization workflows once data ages out.
- **Data Subject Requests**: If a user requests to see or delete their data, you must locate it across all microservices, verifying identity and ensuring full compliance. A centralized user data directory or consistent user ID across services helps streamline these processes.

Mobile-Specific Edge Cases: Certain data might remain on user devices, beyond direct server control. Clearly inform users which data remains client-side vs. server-side, especially if you must remove personally identifying info upon request.

8.5 Auditability and Logging for Security

While **Chapter 7** focused on observability from an operational standpoint, here we consider **security logging** specifically:

8.5.1 Differentiating Application Logs from Security Logs

- **Application Logs**: Typically record business logic events, error traces, performance data.
- **Security Logs**: More specialized, capturing authentication attempts, permission checks, suspicious activity (e.g., repeated 401 responses from the same IP).
- **Audit Logs**: A subset of security logs that are legally or regulatorily mandated, providing a tamper-evident record of critical events (e.g., changes to user privileges, financial transactions).

8.5.2 Ensuring Integrity and Non-Repudiation

Non-repudiation means users cannot deny they performed an action if the logs prove otherwise, or an administrator cannot tamper with logs to hide wrongdoing. Strategies:

- **Digital Signatures**: Each log entry is signed, or entire log files are hashed with a chain-like structure (similar to blockchain concepts).

- **Write-Once Storage**: Some systems physically or logically prevent modifications (e.g., Amazon S3 with Object Lock in compliance mode).
- **Time-Stamping Authority**: For extremely sensitive contexts, an external trusted authority can timestamp log entries.

8.5.3 Access Controls over Logs

Ensure that only authorized personnel (e.g., security admins, compliance officers) can view or export security logs. Overly broad access can risk insider threats or accidental data leaks. Implement:

- **Role-Based Access Control (RBAC)** on log management tools.
- **Segregation of Duties**: Admins who can alter production systems might not have permission to delete or modify security logs.

8.6 Emerging Threats and Advanced Security Topics

The security landscape evolves constantly. Microservices for mobile apps can be exposed to novel attack vectors if not continually updated.

8.6.1 Supply Chain Risks

If you rely on open-source libraries, container images, or third-party dependencies, supply chain compromises can embed malicious code:

- **Dependency Scanning**: Tools like **Snyk**, **Dependabot**, or **Trivy** automatically detect known vulnerabilities in containers and libraries.
- **Signature Verification**: Signed container images and SBOMs (Software Bill of Materials) help ensure the code you run is what you expect.
- **Isolated Build Environments**: Use ephemeral CI/CD environments where external dependencies are pinned to specific versions or checksums.

8.6.2 DevSecOps and Security Automation

DevSecOps integrates security checks into every stage of development:

- **Static Application Security Testing (SAST)**: Scans code for vulnerabilities (e.g., buffer overflows, SQL injection).
- **Dynamic Application Security Testing (DAST)**: Probes a running service for vulnerabilities. Tools like **OWASP ZAP** can automate scans.
- **Infrastructure as Code (IaC) Security**: Tools scan Terraform, Kubernetes manifests, or Dockerfiles for misconfigurations (e.g., public S3 buckets).

- **Policy as Code**: Use frameworks like **Open Policy Agent (OPA)** to define and enforce security rules across microservices.

8.6.3 Penetration Testing and Bug Bounties

Proactively test your microservices architecture:

1. **Penetration Testing**: Hire or maintain an internal "red team" that attempts real-world attacks. They might exploit insufficient input validation, missing encryption, or open ports in your infrastructure.
2. **Bug Bounty Programs**: Incentivize security researchers to responsibly disclose vulnerabilities. Best suited for well-established apps with dedicated triage processes.

8.6.4 Real-Time Threat Detection and WAF

- **Web Application Firewall (WAF)**: Inspect incoming traffic for malicious patterns (SQL injection, XSS).
- **Runtime Application Self-Protection (RASP)**: Embeds security checks inside the application runtime.
- **Machine Learning**: Some advanced solutions detect anomalies in real-time, such as unusual request patterns from a single IP or abrupt spikes in privileged API calls.
- **Threat Intelligence**: Integrating feeds that identify known malicious IPs or user agents. If your microservices see repeated hits from such sources, automatically block or require additional verification.

In conclusion, Security and Compliance presents a holistic framework for protecting microservices that power mobile applications—covering user authentication, service-to-service encryption, data protection, regulatory obligations, and advanced security practices. The multi-layered nature of mobile microservices means each layer (device, network, microservice, data store) must be hardened. Combining robust **authentication/authorization** protocols (JWT, OAuth 2.0, SSO), **service-to-service encryption** (mTLS), secure **data management** (encryption at rest, secrets vaults), and thorough **compliance** measures (GDPR, HIPAA, PCI-DSS) establishes a strong baseline.

Chapter 9: Performance Tuning and Scalability

Microservices for mobile applications must handle unpredictable load patterns. One moment, usage is moderate; the next, a viral marketing campaign or a global push notification can spike traffic exponentially. Beyond raw capacity, users demand low-latency responses. If one microservice in the chain lags, the entire user experience can suffer—leading to lost engagement or revenue. Hence, robust **performance tuning** and **scalability** practices are vital.

9.1 Scaling Microservices for Variable Mobile Loads

9.1.1 Horizontal vs. Vertical Scaling Approaches

Scaling means making more system resources available to handle increased load. Two traditional strategies:

1. **Vertical Scaling**: Adding more CPU, memory, or disk capacity to an existing server or container. For instance, changing an EC2 instance from a `t3.medium` to an `m5.large`.
   - **Advantages**: Simple to implement initially. No code changes required.
   - **Drawbacks**: Eventually hits physical limits. A single instance can become a single point of failure if it goes down.
2. **Horizontal Scaling**: Adding more instances (or replicas) of a microservice. A load balancer or orchestrator distributes traffic among them.
   - **Advantages**: Often more fault-tolerant, can scale out almost indefinitely if stateless or well-partitioned.

- ○ **Drawbacks**: Requires architecture that supports distributed state (e.g., external caches, partitioned databases). Some complexities arise when synchronizing sessions or data across multiple instances.

For **mobile** workloads—where traffic can spike unpredictably—**horizontal scaling** is more common. Microservices that are stateless can spin up multiple containers or serverless functions to meet demand, then scale back down when traffic subsides, optimizing costs.

Example: Horizontal Scaling in Kubernetes

If your "Notification Service" is containerized, you might define a **Deployment** that starts with two replicas. When CPU usage or request rate surpasses thresholds, an **Horizontal Pod Autoscaler (HPA)** automatically increases replicas:

```
apiVersion: apps/v1

kind: Deployment

metadata:

  name: notification-service

spec:

  replicas: 2

  selector:

    matchLabels:

      app: notification

  template:

    metadata:

      labels:

        app: notification

    spec:

      containers:

      - name: notification-container

        image: myorg/notification-service:1.0

        resources:
```

```yaml
    requests:

      cpu: "250m"

      memory: "256Mi"

    limits:

      cpu: "500m"

      memory: "512Mi"


------

apiVersion: autoscaling/v2

kind: HorizontalPodAutoscaler

metadata:

 name: notification-hpa

spec:

 scaleTargetRef:

  apiVersion: apps/v1

  kind: Deployment

  name: notification-service

 minReplicas: 2

 maxReplicas: 10

 metrics:

  - type: Resource

   resource:

    name: cpu

    target:

     type: Utilization

     averageUtilization: 70
```

When average CPU usage crosses 70% across the current pods, Kubernetes spins up additional replicas (up to 10). This is vital in a scenario where a mass push notification to millions of mobile devices triggers a flood of read/write requests.

9.1.2 Auto-Scaling Policies for Traffic Spikes

In addition to resource-based triggers (CPU, memory), more advanced policies can use:

- **Request Rate**: E.g., scale up if requests per second exceed 500 across all pods.
- **Latency**: If p95 latency climbs above 300ms, scale out to reduce queue time.
- **Custom Business Metrics**: For a shopping app, scale up if "items added to cart per minute" surges, anticipating an eventual purchase load.

Mobile-Specific: The load might come in short bursts—for instance, when users in one time zone finish work or respond to a push. Tune auto-scaling "cooldown" periods to avoid thrashing. Some orchestrators or serverless platforms handle bursting better than others.

9.1.3 Strategies for Stateful or Legacy Services

While many microservices are stateless by design, certain stateful components (like an old monolith or a specialized data store) can be harder to scale horizontally. Options:

- **Partitioning**: Split data by region, user ID range, or usage pattern (sharding).
- **Migration to Managed Services**: Use a cloud-based database with built-in scaling (e.g., Amazon DynamoDB, Google Spanner).
- **Caching**: Offload read-intensive queries to Redis or an in-memory layer, reducing the load on the stateful backend.

Gradual refactoring of these stateful components into microservices that are more easily horizontally scalable is often beneficial in the long term.

9.2 Load Balancing and Traffic Management

9.2.1 Routing Strategies and Service Discovery

Load balancers evenly distribute incoming requests among multiple instances of a microservice. In a containerized environment (e.g., Kubernetes), the Service object or Ingress might handle basic distribution. Outside of K8s, you might rely on NGINX, HAProxy, or cloud load balancers (AWS ALB, GCP Load Balancing).

Routing can be:

1. **Round Robin**: Requests go to each instance in turn. Simple but doesn't account for differences in instance load.
2. **Least Connections**: Traffic is sent to the instance with the fewest active connections, improving fairness.
3. **Weighted Round Robin**: Some instances get a higher share of traffic based on capacity or cost.
4. **IP Hash**: Sticky sessions by client IP, though not always recommended for stateless microservices.

Service Discovery solutions (like **Consul**, **Eureka**, or **Kubernetes DNS**) ensure microservices can locate each other dynamically, registering new instances automatically.

Diagram: High-Level Load Balancing

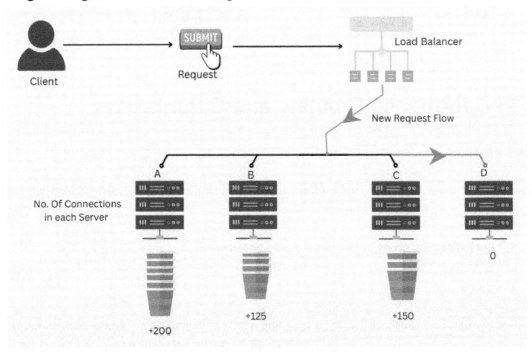

9.2.2 Handling Latency and Regional Deployments

For **global mobile** apps, users might be spread across continents. Minimizing **latency** is paramount:

- **Geo-Distributed Deployments**: Host microservices in multiple regions. A global load balancer routes the user's request to the nearest region.
- **DNS-Based Latency Routing**: Tools like AWS Route 53 can route to the region with the lowest latency automatically.
- **Read-Only Edge Caches**: Common for serving static data (images, configurations), but can also serve precomputed responses for certain microservices (e.g., feed data).

Challenge: Maintaining data consistency across multiple regions. Eventual consistency or advanced multi-primary replication strategies are typical. For instance, if a user updates their profile in Europe and then quickly opens the app in Asia, some data might be stale if replication lags.

9.2.3 Advanced Traffic Shaping and Throttling

When dealing with mobile bursts, you may want to **throttle** or **shape** traffic:

- **Rate Limits**: E.g., each user can only make 20 requests per minute on certain endpoints. Prevents DDoS or accidental flooding from buggy clients.
- **Adaptive Throttling**: If a microservice is near capacity, it can signal the gateway to slow down requests or shed load gracefully.
- **Retry and Backoff**: If the microservice rejects requests with a 429 Too Many Requests, well-behaved mobile apps or aggregator services should back off exponentially rather than continuing to hammer.

9.3 Performance Profiling and Optimization

9.3.1 Profiling Microservices with Low Overhead

Profiling means identifying where CPU time, memory allocations, or I/O overhead is spent. For microservices, typical tools include:

- **Java Flight Recorder** or **YourKit** for JVM-based services.
- **Node.js** built-in profiler or tools like **Clinic.js**.
- **Go pprof** for Go services.

A minimal overhead approach is to run sampling profilers in staging or canary environments. You can also attach profilers in production if usage patterns differ from test, but be cautious about overhead.

Example: Node.js CPU Profiler

```
# Start Node.js with --prof

node --prof index.js



# Generate a performance log, then convert it

node --prof-process isolate-0x103801600-12345-v8.log > processed.txt
```

The resulting `processed.txt` reveals function calls consuming the most CPU time. With microservices often waiting on I/O, you may discover inefficiencies in how your code handles concurrency or external requests.

9.3.2 Identifying Hot Spots in Critical Service Paths

Hot spots occur where your microservices are slowed down by:

1. **Excessive Database Queries**: N+1 query patterns or unoptimized indexing.
2. **Synchronous External Calls**: Some microservices might block while waiting for external APIs.
3. **Inefficient Data Structures**: Large memory usage or repeated serialization overhead can spike CPU.
4. **Logging Overhead**: Writing too many logs synchronously can degrade performance.

Use **distributed tracing** (covered in Chapter 7) to track request latencies across microservices. Correlate traces with profiling data to see, for example, that 70% of time in "OrdersService" is spent building large JSON responses, which might be cut down or optimized.

9.3.3 Language- and Runtime-Specific Optimizations

- **Java**: Fine-tune GC algorithms (e.g., G1 vs. ZGC for large heaps), thread pools, and use efficient data structures (e.g., `StringBuilder` for concatenation, concurrent collections).
- **Node.js**: Leverage asynchronous I/O, ensure event loop is not blocked by CPU-heavy tasks. For CPU-bound code, consider worker threads or separate microservices in a different language.
- **Go**: Optimize goroutine usage, reduce lock contention, handle ephemeral memory allocations carefully.
- **Python**: The GIL (Global Interpreter Lock) can limit concurrency; scale horizontally or use multiprocessing for CPU-bound tasks.

Mobile-Specific: Large JSON payloads and repeated serialization can hamper performance under poor network conditions. Consider binary formats (MessagePack, ProtoBuf) if feasible, or optimize the data shape so the mobile client fetches only the needed fields (GraphQL partial queries, for example).

9.3.4 Performance Budgeting and Reducing Payload Sizes

Define a **performance budget** for each microservice endpoint. For instance, "All requests to `/api/v1/posts` must complete under 200ms p95 on average data volumes." If the payload is too large:

- **Pagination**: Send only partial data.
- **Compression**: GZIP or Brotli. However, note CPU overhead for compression at scale—monitor the trade-off.
- **Binary Protocols**: gRPC or Avro for smaller wire footprints, especially beneficial in mobile contexts.

9.4 Caching and Edge Computing

9.4.1 Edge Services for Near-Real-Time Responses

Edge computing places caching or compute resources closer to end users, reducing round-trip latency. A typical scenario is a **CDN** (Content Delivery Network) that caches static assets or pre-rendered content near major geographic regions.

For microservices, edge nodes can also run simple logic—like an aggregator that merges multiple microservices' data, or a specialized filter that blocks suspicious requests. Some providers (e.g., Cloudflare Workers, AWS Lambda@Edge) let you deploy custom code globally.

Use Cases:

- **Mobile Feeds**: Serving the top items from an edge cache if they rarely change.
- **Location-Based Data**: An edge node in Asia might have cached data for local users, preventing repeated calls to a distant US region.
- **API Gateway at Edge**: Minimizing cross-region round trips.

9.4.2 CDN Integration for Large Media Assets

Many mobile apps store images, videos, or documents that can be heavy on bandwidth. For microservices, offloading this static content to a CDN drastically reduces load. Implementation steps:

1. **Upload**: The microservice or user uploads media to cloud storage (e.g., S3).
2. **CDN Distribution**: The cloud storage is fronted by a CDN. The microservice references the CDN URL in its responses.
3. **Cache Invalidation**: If an asset updates, the microservice triggers a CDN invalidation or uses versioned filenames.

This approach decouples large media traffic from your microservices, freeing them to focus on dynamic logic.

9.4.3 Microservice-Level Caching

Some dynamic data can also be cached. Examples:

- **In-Memory Caches**: E.g., Redis or Memcached. The microservice checks Redis before hitting a database or external API.
- **HTTP Response Caching**: Microservices might set Cache-Control headers, letting the mobile app or intermediary caches store responses for a short TTL.

Challenges: Stale data, invalidation complexity, and concurrency issues if multiple microservices or clients update data simultaneously. Patterns like event-driven invalidation or short TTL can help keep caches correct while still providing performance benefits.

9.5 Concurrency and Resource Utilization

9.5.1 Concurrency Models in Popular Microservice Runtimes

Each runtime (Java, Node.js, Go, Python, .NET) has unique concurrency patterns:

- **Java**: Typically uses thread pools (e.g., Executors.newFixedThreadPool) or reactive libraries like Vert.x or Spring WebFlux.
- **Node.js**: Single-threaded event loop. CPU-intensive tasks must be offloaded to worker threads or separate microservices.
- **Go**: Lightweight goroutines with a built-in scheduler. Potentially large concurrency with minimal overhead.
- **Python**: The GIL can hamper multi-threaded CPU concurrency, so solutions include multiprocessing or asynchronous frameworks (e.g., asyncio) for I/O-bound tasks.

Mobile Use Case: The biggest concurrency challenge often arises from an avalanche of short-lived requests, especially if the user base is large. Efficiently handling I/O-bound tasks (e.g., database queries, external calls) is crucial. Synchronous blocking can cause thread starvation or blocked event loops.

Sample Code: Node.js Worker Threads for CPU-Bound

```
// heavyTask.js

const { parentPort } = require('worker_threads');


parentPort.on('message', (data) => {

  // CPU-intensive operation, e.g., image processing
```

```
  const result = doHeavyComputation(data);

  parentPort.postMessage(result);

});


// mainService.js
const { Worker } = require('worker_threads');


function handleRequest(req, res) {

  const worker = new Worker('./heavyTask.js');

  worker.on('message', (result) => {

    res.json({ processed: result });

  });

  worker.postMessage(req.body.payload);

}
```

This approach prevents the main event loop from stalling while a CPU-intensive task runs, improving concurrency for large numbers of mobile requests.

9.5.2 Resource Allocation and Ephemeral Compute

Ephemeral compute refers to short-lived resources that scale up and down on demand, such as AWS Fargate tasks, Azure Container Instances, or Google Cloud Run. These platforms can automatically run more instances of your container to meet spikes in traffic, then spin them down when idle.

- **Pros**: Eliminates the need to manage servers or pre-warm container fleets.
- **Cons**: Potential cold starts if your code or container image is large.
- **Optimizations**: Keep container images minimal, reduce initialization overhead, possibly keep small baseline capacity running to mitigate cold starts.

9.5.3 Bulkhead Isolation to Prevent Resource Contention

Bulkhead partitions resources (thread pools, connection pools) so that a surge in one microservice function doesn't starve others. Example:

- **Payment microservice** can have a dedicated pool of 20 threads for external payment gateway calls. If the payment gateway is slow or partially down, those 20 threads fill up, but the service's other endpoints remain available for tasks like retrieving user payment history.

In container orchestration, you can also allocate CPU or memory limits to ensure no single microservice's containers starve others. This prevents meltdown scenarios under heavy load from a single feature.

9.6 Emerging Trends in Performance and Scalability

9.6.1 eBPF-Based Telemetry and Optimizations

Extended Berkeley Packet Filter (eBPF) allows you to run sandboxed programs in the Linux kernel, enabling advanced telemetry and performance tuning without instrumentation in code. Tools like **Cilium** or **Pixie** use eBPF to gather real-time metrics about network calls, CPU usage, or kernel events. Potential microservice applications:

- **Network Profiling**: Identify the slowest calls or highest-latency cross-service communications at the socket level.
- **Runtime Security**: eBPF can block suspicious syscalls.
- **Zero-Overhead Observability**: Minimizes overhead compared to in-process profiling.

While eBPF is advanced, it's gaining traction in high-performance microservice environments.

9.6.2 Advanced Serverless Concurrency

Serverless platforms are evolving to handle concurrency more gracefully:

- **AWS Lambda Provisioned Concurrency**: Minlmizes cold starts by keeping pre-initlalized environments ready.
- **Cloudflare Workers**: Lightweight JavaScript environments that spawn instantly near the user edge.
- **Azure Functions Premium Plan**: Offers higher concurrency and memory while maintaining auto-scaling.

For mobile applications with spiky usage, an advanced serverless approach can yield cost savings yet handle bursts. The key is monitoring concurrency limits, ensuring you do not exceed free or default quotas unexpectedly.

9.6.3 GPU-Accelerated or Specialized Hardware Microservices

As ML and heavy computation become more common in mobile apps (e.g., real-time translation, image recognition), some microservices may require GPU acceleration or specialized hardware (TPUs, FPGAs). Container orchestration platforms increasingly support GPU scheduling:

```
apiVersion: apps/v1

kind: Deployment

metadata:

  name: image-processing-service

spec:

  template:

    spec:

      containers:

      - name: image-processor

        image: myorg/gpu-image-processor:latest

        resources:

          limits:

            nvidia.com/gpu: 1
```

This ensures the container only runs on nodes with GPU resources. Performance for certain tasks (like large-scale image classification) can improve drastically. For routine microservices, CPU-based scaling remains sufficient, but specialized hardware is an emerging area for performance boosts.

9.6.4 Unikernels and MicroVMs

Some organizations experiment with **unikernels** or **microVMs** (e.g., **Firecracker**) for ultra-fast startup times and minimal overhead. Instead of running a full OS in each container, you compile just the necessary OS components with your application. This approach can yield:

- **Faster Cold Starts**: Boot times in milliseconds.
- **Reduced Attack Surface**: Fewer OS components.
- **Higher Density**: Fit more microVMs on the same hardware.

However, unikernel ecosystems are still evolving, and the tooling can be less mature than

Docker containers. This is an area to watch if you need extremely high concurrency with ephemeral spin-ups.

9.7 Case Study: Scaling a Social Media Feed Service

To concretize these ideas, consider a **social media feed** microservice that must handle a large volume of read requests from mobile clients. Each read merges data from user profiles, posts, and analytics for personalization. Over time, traffic has grown, and peak usage periods see latency spikes. A path to improved performance and scalability might include:

1. **Edge Caching**: Caching the "top posts" globally, so most read requests are served near-instantly from a CDN.
2. **Async Data Aggregation**: Splitting the microservice into smaller ones: "ProfileService," "PostService," "AnalyticsService." A background job aggregates a feed, storing partial data in Redis for quick retrieval.
3. **Horizontal Scaling**: Deploy multiple instances of the "FeedAggregatorService." Use HPA based on CPU usage or number of queued tasks.
4. **Profiling**: Identify that 40% of time is spent merging user profile pictures. Convert to an asynchronous call or pre-fetch in a caching layer.
5. **Bulkhead Pattern**: Isolate feed read calls from feed write calls. If writes to the database are delayed, reads remain unaffected.
6. **Global Load Balancing**: Deploy in multiple regions, letting each region handle local user requests. Replicate data asynchronously.

Performance metrics reveal p95 latency dropping from 600ms to 200ms, while the system handles 2-3x the traffic after implementing these changes.

9.8 Final Reflections on Performance and Scalability

Performance tuning and scalability form a continuous journey rather than a one-time task. For **mobile-first** microservices:

- **Bursty Load**: Expect and prepare for abrupt spikes, employing auto-scaling triggers that respond quickly.
- **Efficient Payloads**: Large or unnecessary data transmissions cost user time and degrade app reviews.
- **Global Footprint**: Latency matters. Deploy microservices or caches near your largest user bases.
- **Continuous Profiling**: Tools like distributed tracing, eBPF, or runtime profilers help you find new bottlenecks as the system evolves.
- **Cost vs. Performance**: Over-provisioning to handle extreme peaks can be expensive;

Chapter 10: Testing and Quality Assurance

Building microservices to support a mobile application involves multiple teams, services, and release cycles, often with high user expectations and rapidly evolving features. Achieving consistent quality requires a well-defined **testing strategy** that covers:

1. **Unit and Integration Testing**: Ensuring each microservice's internal logic and its interactions with immediate dependencies work correctly.
2. **Contract Testing Across Multiple Services**: Verifying that microservices agree on API contracts, preventing regressions or breaking changes in a distributed environment.
3. **End-to-End Testing in a Mobile Context**: Simulating user flows from a mobile device's perspective, including network constraints and device quirks.
4. **Chaos Engineering and Reliability Testing**: Introducing controlled failure scenarios to confirm resilience, crucial for microservices that must handle intermittent mobile usage and potentially unreliable networks.
5. **Test Data Management and Environments**: Handling ephemeral test data, realistic test scenarios, and environment parity (e.g., staging vs. production).
6. **Automation and CI/CD Integration**: Embedding tests into continuous integration and continuous deployment pipelines, ensuring rapid feedback for dev teams.

10.1 Unit and Integration Testing

10.1.1 Test Automation for Microservices APIs

Unit testing focuses on verifying the smallest units of code—classes, functions, or components—while integration testing verifies how these pieces work together, including external dependencies like databases, message queues, or third-party APIs. Because microservices are often exposed as APIs, robust test automation is critical for capturing issues early.

Typical Testing Stack:

- **Language-Specific Test Framework**: e.g., **Jest** for Node.js, **JUnit** for Java, **pytest** for Python, **Go testing** for Go.
- **Mocking/Stubbing Tools**: e.g., **Sinon** for JavaScript, **unittest.mock** for Python, **Mockito** for Java.
- **Assertion Libraries**: Usually built-in, or extended frameworks like **Chai** for JavaScript, **Hamcrest** for Java.

Example: Node.js Unit Test with Jest

```
// userService.js

async function getUser(userId, db) {

  const user = await db.findOne({ _id: userId });

  if (!user) throw new Error('User not found');

  return user;

}


module.exports = { getUser };


// userService.test.js

const { getUser } = require('./userService');


test('getUser returns user if found in db', async () => {

  const mockDb = {

    findOne: jest.fn().mockResolvedValue({ _id: 'abc123', name: 'Alice' })

  };
```

```
  const result = await getUser('abc123', mockDb);

  expect(result).toEqual({ _id: 'abc123', name: 'Alice' });

});


test('getUser throws error if user not found', async () => {

  const mockDb = {

    findOne: jest.fn().mockResolvedValue(null)

  };


  await expect(getUser('nonexistent', mockDb)).rejects.toThrow('User not found');

});
```

Key Points:

- The db dependency is **mocked**, so the test focuses on logic rather than external resources.
- Each test scenario is explicit and independent.

10.1.2 Contract Testing Across Multiple Services

Although contract testing is sometimes treated separately, it also falls under integration testing. **Contract tests** confirm that providers (e.g., a microservice exposing an API) and consumers (e.g., another microservice calling that API) share consistent expectations about request/response formats. This is essential in microservices for mobile, where frequent updates risk breaking older client versions.

A popular approach is **Pact** (or similar frameworks), which automates contract tests:

1. **Consumer Tests**: The consumer microservice runs tests that generate a **Pact file** (JSON) describing expected interactions.
2. **Provider Verification**: The provider microservice runs a verifier against the Pact file to ensure it can produce the responses the consumer expects.

Pact Example

Consumer-Side (Node.js consumer tests)

```javascript
// consumer.spec.js
const { Pact } = require('@pact-foundation/pact');

const { expect } = require('chai');

const { fetchUser } = require('./consumerClient');


describe('UserService consumer', () => {
  const provider = new Pact({
    consumer: 'OrderService',
    provider: 'UserService',
    port: 1234,
  });


  before(() => provider.setup());
  after(() => provider.finalize());


  describe('when a request for a user is made', () => {
    before(() =>
      provider.addInteraction({
        state: 'User exists',
        uponReceiving: 'a GET request for user',
        withRequest: {
          method: 'GET',
          path: '/users/abc123',
        },
        willRespondWith: {
```

```
      status: 200,

      headers: { 'Content-Type': 'application/json' },

      body: {

        _id: 'abc123',

        name: 'Alice',

      },

    },

  })

);


  it('returns the user', async () => {

    const user = await fetchUser('abc123', 'http://localhost:1234');

    expect(user).to.deep.equal({ _id: 'abc123', name: 'Alice' });

  });

  });

});
```

Provider-Side (verifying Pact)

```
pact-provider-verifier \

  --provider-base-url=http://localhost:3000 \

  --pact-urls=./pacts/order_service-user_service.json \

  --publish-verification-results \

  --provider-version=1.0.0
```

If the provider's actual responses match the contract, verification succeeds. Otherwise, the pipeline fails, preventing a breaking change from being deployed.

10.1.3 Collaboration Between Teams for Test Coverage

Microservices often involve multiple squads (e.g., "User Team," "Billing Team"). Each must define a clear **API contract**. Over time, these squads collaborate:

- **Shared Repositories**: Hosting contract definitions or OpenAPI specs in a central location.
- **Design Reviews**: Early feedback loops when new endpoints or data fields are introduced.
- **Automated Checks**: Each microservice's CI pipeline includes consumer-driven contract tests for immediate feedback.

By systematically capturing expectations, teams reduce costly integration bugs and maintain a stable mobile user experience despite frequent backend changes.

10.2 End-to-End Testing in a Mobile Environment

10.2.1 Simulating Real User Flows and Network Conditions

End-to-end (E2E) testing ensures the **entire system** works from the mobile user's perspective. For example, a test might:

1. Install the mobile app (or run it in a simulator/emulator).
2. Interact with the UI (tap "Login," enter credentials).
3. Call multiple microservices behind the scenes.
4. Verify correct app states or server responses.

Network conditions matter. Mobile devices may have **limited bandwidth** or **high latency**. Tools like **Network Link Conditioner** (iOS), **Android's emulator network settings**, or advanced solutions (e.g., **Charles Proxy**, **Postman** with throttling) can simulate poor connections or packet loss. This is crucial for verifying offline flows or ensuring microservices gracefully handle timeouts.

Example: Automated Mobile E2E with Appium

Appium is an open-source framework for automating mobile app testing on iOS, Android, or hybrid apps.

```
// e2eTest.js

const wdio = require("webdriverio");
```

```
const opts = {

 path: '/wd/hub',

 port: 4723,

 capabilities: {

  platformName: "Android",

  deviceName: "Android Emulator",

  app: "/path/to/mobileApp.apk"

 }

};


(async () => {

 const client = await wdio.remote(opts);


 // Simulate user tapping the "Login" button

 const loginButton = await client.$("~loginButton");

 await loginButton.click();


 // Enter credentials

 const usernameField = await client.$("~username");

 await usernameField.setValue("testUser");

 const passwordField = await client.$("~password");

 await passwordField.setValue("secretPass");


 // Submit login

 const submitBtn = await client.$("~submit");
```

```
await submitBtn.click();


// Validate success by checking for a user profile element

const profileElem = await client.$("~profileScreen");

const isDisplayed = await profileElem.isDisplayed();

console.log("Profile screen displayed:", isDisplayed);


await client.deleteSession();
})();
```

In parallel, you can configure network shaping on the emulator to simulate 3G speeds or intermittent drops, verifying the microservices' resilience and the app's offline caching logic.

10.2.2 Testing Across Different Mobile Platforms

Android and **iOS** each have distinct UI patterns, OS versions, and hardware differences. For thorough coverage:

- **Android Varieties**: Different manufacturers, screen sizes, CPU architectures.
- **iOS Versions**: Apple's older OS versions still in use. Each OS update can introduce subtle changes in app behavior.
- **Device Farms**: Services like **AWS Device Farm**, **BrowserStack**, or **Sauce Labs** host real devices. Automated tests run across dozens of device/OS combinations, capturing logs, screenshots, or videos.

Microservices rarely differ by device platform, but real user interactions may cause distinct request patterns or concurrency. For example, iOS might handle push notifications differently from Android, requiring separate E2E scenarios.

10.2.3 Testing Offline Scenarios and Data Synchronization

Mobile apps often support offline usage. Suppose a user modifies data while offline, then reconnects. The backend microservices must handle replayed requests, merges, or conflict resolution. E2E tests might:

1. Launch the app with normal connectivity, authenticate, and fetch initial data.
2. Disable network or throttle to a near-zero rate.

148

3. Perform offline actions (e.g., create a draft post).
4. Re-enable network; verify data syncs to the microservices, ensuring the final state is consistent.

Challenges:

- **Complex Data Merge**: If the user also changed the same data from another device while offline, your microservices might have conflicting versions.
- **Eventual Consistency**: E2E tests must wait for asynchronous updates or poll the microservices for updated state.

10.3 Contract Testing and API Backward Compatibility

Although we briefly covered contract testing, it deserves separate emphasis for **backward compatibility**—critical in mobile environments, where older app versions linger in production for months or years. An API change that breaks older clients can cause widespread disruption.

10.3.1 Versioning Strategies

Common versioning patterns for microservices:

- **URL-Based**: e.g., `/api/v2/users` for a new version.
- **Header-Based**: e.g., `Accept: application/vnd.myapp+json;version=2`.
- **GraphQL Schema Versioning**: Mark fields as deprecated, remove them after a grace period.

Each approach requires robust testing:

- **Can older versions still call the new API without errors?**
- **Do new fields remain optional to avoid breaking older client code?**

10.3.2 Automated Verification of Deprecated Endpoints

When microservices deprecate or remove an endpoint, test suites should confirm:

1. The endpoint still works for older clients until the official removal date.
2. The microservice logs usage of deprecated endpoints, so QA can see if significant traffic persists, indicating users haven't upgraded.
3. A "sunset date" or other header informs clients about impending removal.

Example: A contract test for a soon-to-be-deprecated field `email` ensures the provider microservice still includes emai l in the response for older client versions. Once usage dips below a threshold, you can remove the field—after verifying no major client versions rely on it.

10.4 Chaos Engineering and Reliability Testing

10.4.1 Injecting Failures into the System

Microservices benefit from **chaos engineering**—proactively introducing controlled failures (e.g., network timeouts, server crashes) to confirm resilience. This is especially relevant for mobile apps, where partial connectivity or spikes in traffic can cause components to fail.

Chaos engineering tools include:

- **Chaos Monkey** (originally by Netflix): Randomly terminates instances in production.
- **Gremlin**, **Litmus**: Commercial or open-source chaos platforms with user-friendly UIs to craft experiments (like CPU hog, memory spikes, DNS blackholes).
- **Kubernetes**: You can inject ephemeral sidecars to sabotage pods or pods themselves to simulate container restarts.

Example: Fault Injection with Gremlin

```
# Launch a CPU attack on a microservice labeled "billing"

gremlin attack --target=billing --cpu 90 --length 300
```

This simulates 90% CPU usage for 5 minutes. QA observes whether the "BillingService" auto-scales or if requests to "PaymentService" degrade. The system's logs and metrics reveal if fallback or circuit breakers engaged.

10.4.2 Monitoring System Behavior Under Stress

Chaos experiments must include thorough monitoring:

1. **Define Hypothesis**: e.g., "If the BillingService CPU is maxed, PaymentService calls degrade, but the rest of the system remains functional."
2. **Run Experiment**: Induce CPU usage spike.
3. **Observe Metrics and Logs**: Look for higher error rates, longer latencies, or partial failures.
4. **Postmortem**: If real user traffic would have been impacted severely, you found a resilience gap. Improve the microservice or implement fallback behaviors.

10.4.3 Automated Resilience Testing in CI/CD

While chaos engineering is often associated with production, smaller scale experiments can run in a staging environment. For instance:

- **Automated scenario**: Spin up a full staging cluster, run E2E tests while injecting random pod failures for 15 minutes.
- If any critical path test fails, the pipeline blocks the release.

This approach ensures each new version meets baseline resilience criteria before shipping.

10.5 Test Data Management and Environments

10.5.1 Simulating Production-Like Conditions

Microservices rely on data from various databases, caches, or external APIs. Testing in an environment that's too artificial can miss real-world edge cases. Yet, copying production data can raise **privacy** or **compliance** issues. Solutions:

- **Synthetic Data Generation**: Use scripts to generate realistic but fake user records, transactions, or logs. Tools like **Mockaroo**, **Faker**, or custom code can produce large volumes with plausible distribution patterns.
- **Anonymized Production Clones**: If permitted, you can clone production data, then anonymize or obfuscate PII fields before using it in QA. For instance, real user emails replaced with placeholders, real names replaced with random strings.

Mobile-Specific: Make sure test data includes a wide range of device usage patterns—some users might have partial profile info, some might have large media attachments, etc.

10.5.2 Ephemeral Test Environments

Rather than a single staging environment, many teams spin up ephemeral environments on demand. For instance, when a developer opens a pull request, the CI pipeline:

1. Creates a temporary environment (e.g., using **Helm** or **Terraform**).
2. Deploys the microservice changes plus dependencies.
3. Runs integration or E2E tests with seeded test data.
4. Tears down the environment when done.

Example: Script for Ephemeral Environment

```bash
#!/usr/bin/env bash


export ENV_NAME="pr-123"

echo "Creating ephemeral environment $ENV_NAME..."


# (Pseudo-commands)

helm install user-service --set image.tag=pr-123 --namespace=$ENV_NAME

helm install order-service --set image.tag=pr-123 --namespace=$ENV_NAME


# Wait for readiness

kubectl wait --for=condition=available deployment/user-service -n $ENV_NAME


# Run test suite

npm run e2e-tests -- --endpoint=https://$ENV_NAME.mycompany.internal


echo "Tearing down environment..."

helm uninstall user-service --namespace=$ENV_NAME

helm uninstall order-service --namespace=$ENV_NAME

kubectl delete namespace $ENV_NAME
```

This ensures minimal collisions among parallel merges, letting QA or dev teams see precisely how the updated microservice behaves in near-isolation.

10.5.3 Data Cleanup and Test Repeatability

Repeated test runs can pollute databases, leading to inconsistent states (e.g., leftover user records, partial orders). Solutions:

- **Rollback/Truncate** after tests: Each test environment is ephemeral or each test run cleans up data.

- **Idempotent Data Setup**: The same test can run multiple times without side effects, often by resetting the database schema or using unique keys.
- **Dockerized Database**: Spin up a fresh container for each test run, seeded with test fixtures.

10.6 Automation and CI/CD Integration

10.6.1 Automating Builds, Tests, and Deployments

A robust testing strategy means little if not automated in a **continuous integration/continuous deployment (CI/CD)** pipeline. Each commit triggers:

1. **Unit Tests**: Quick feedback, often within seconds or minutes.
2. **Integration & Contract Tests**: Verifies microservices or external APIs.
3. **E2E Tests**: Possibly in a separate stage due to longer runtime.
4. **Manual Approval or Automatic Deployment**: If all tests pass, the microservice can be deployed to staging or production.

For microservices, each repository might have its own pipeline, or a monorepo approach might run partial pipelines for changed services. Tools like **Jenkins**, **GitLab CI**, **GitHub Actions**, or **CircleCI** are commonly used.

Example: GitHub Actions Workflow

```
name: CI


on:
  push:
    branches: [ "main" ]


jobs:
  build-and-test:
    runs-on: ubuntu-latest
    steps:
      - uses: actions/checkout@v2
```

```
- name: Install dependencies

  run: npm install

- name: Run unit tests

  run: npm test

- name: Run contract tests

  run: npm run contract-tests

- name: Build container

  run: docker build -t myorg/microservice:${{ github.sha }} .

- name: Push to registry

  run: |

    docker login ...

    docker push myorg/microservice:${{ github.sha }}
```

10.6.2 Pipeline Strategies for Large Mobile-Focused Apps

When mobile features change rapidly, you might push microservice updates weekly or even daily. Avoid pipeline bottlenecks by:

- **Parallelization**: Unit tests, integration tests, and contract tests run in parallel. E2E might run in a separate pipeline or after partial acceptance.
- **Selective Testing**: If only the "User Service" changed, skip E2E tests that revolve around "Notifications Service." Some caution is needed to not skip needed cross-service tests.
- **Canary or Blue-Green Deployments**: Deploy changes to a small subset of users or a separate environment, run additional tests, then roll forward if stable.

10.6.3 Reporting and Visibility

Clear feedback loops help QA and dev teams track quality trends:

- **Dashboards**: Show test pass/fail rates over time, flakiness metrics, coverage stats.
- **Slack/Email Notifications**: Real-time alerts if a critical test fails on main or in a staging environment.
- **Test Coverage Tools**: Tools like **Istanbul/nyc** (for JS), **Jacoco** (Java), or **coverage.py** (Python) highlight untested code areas, guiding QA focus.

10.7 Real-World Scenarios and Best Practices

10.7.1 Handling Flaky Tests

Flaky tests pass or fail inconsistently, often due to concurrency, timing, or external dependencies. They can erode trust in automation. Solutions:

- **Stabilize Setup**: Wait for microservices to be ready, or mock out unreliable external calls.
- **Isolate Timers/Async**: Avoid test timeouts that are too tight. Use explicit waiting or polling for certain conditions.
- **Retry Logic**: Mark certain tests "retryable" if they fail for known transient reasons, but do so sparingly.
- **Pin External Versions**: If an external API changes unpredictably, consider a dedicated mock or test environment with fixed responses.

10.7.2 Security Testing as Part of QA

Even though security is its own domain, basic **security checks** often appear in QA:

- **Static Analysis**: Tools can catch dangerous patterns (like SQL injection) in code.
- **Dependency Vulnerabilities**: Automated scans for outdated libraries.
- **Basic Pen Tests**: QA might attempt injecting malicious input or unauthorized endpoints.
- **API Fuzzing**: Tools generate random inputs to find possible crashes or unhandled edge cases.

10.7.3 Cross-Team Coordination for Mobile Releases

Mobile apps often have front-end changes that need new or updated microservice endpoints. Meanwhile, older app versions may still rely on older endpoints. QA processes can:

1. **Link Git Commits**: The front-end code merges referencing the back-end merges, so testers know which versions correspond.
2. **Feature Flags**: Release new features behind flags so QA can enable or disable them in staging.
3. **Release Trains**: If multiple microservices must go live simultaneously for a new user flow, a "release train" model coordinates deployment and testing windows.

10.7.4 E2E Testing with Mocked External Dependencies

If your microservices call external APIs (payments, geolocation, social media), you may not want to rely on those in test environments. Instead:

- **WireMock** or **MockServer** can simulate external endpoints with predictable responses or error conditions.
- For final stage tests, you might have a dedicated sandbox account on a real external API. Ensure you handle rate limits or ephemeral data.

10.8 Putting It All Together

Imagine a scenario where your mobile app offers **on-demand services** (e.g., ride-sharing, food delivery). The microservices might be:

- **UserService** (manages user profiles and authentication)
- **OrderService** (handles orders, from creation to completion)
- **PaymentService** (integrates with payment gateways)
- **NotificationService** (push notifications, messaging)

A comprehensive QA strategy:

1. **Unit Tests**: Each service has a suite verifying core logic (e.g., calculating ride fares, verifying valid addresses).
2. **Contract Tests**: The **PaymentService** ensures it still meets the **OrderService** expectations for charging or refunding transactions, even if PaymentService updates its response schema.
3. **E2E Mobile Tests**: Using Appium, QA verifies a user can open the app, log in, place an order, pay, and receive confirmation. These tests run nightly or before major releases.
4. **Chaos Engineering**: In a staging cluster, randomly kill NotificationService pods or inject payment gateway timeouts. QA verifies that the system recovers gracefully, and the mobile app shows user-friendly errors.
5. **Load/Performance Testing**: Although covered in more detail in performance chapters, QA also runs basic stress tests to ensure OrderService can handle peak demand.
6. **Automated CI/CD**: On each commit to any microservice repo, unit tests and contract tests run. Before merging to main, ephemeral environments spin up for E2E tests. A final gating step includes canary deployment with partial real traffic. If errors remain low, the new version is promoted to all users.

Over time, teams refine coverage, reduce flakiness, and adopt new testing tools or strategies to keep pace with the dynamic nature of mobile usage patterns.

Chapter 11: Real-World Case Studies and Future Directions

Throughout this book, we have covered microservice architecture fundamentals, design strategies, deployment and infrastructure choices, data management, communication patterns, observability, security, performance tuning, and testing—each tailored to **mobile applications**. These topics form a robust framework for building and operating mobile-focused microservices.

In this final chapter, we bring these principles together through **real-world case studies**—demonstrating how actual companies, products, or hypothetical but realistic scenarios overcame unique challenges using microservices to support mobile ecosystems. We then shift our lens to **emerging trends** and **future directions**, highlighting how artificial intelligence (AI), 5G, edge computing, and other evolving technologies may reshape mobile microservice architectures in the years to come.

11.1 Microservices Success Stories in Mobile

11.1.1 E-Commerce App: Scaling During Seasonal Peaks

Company Profile: An online retailer with a popular **mobile shopping app** used across multiple continents. Originally, the retailer ran a monolithic backend hosted on a single data center, but seasonal sales (especially around Black Friday or Singles' Day) led to repeated downtime and poor user experience.

Journey to Microservices

- **Initial Monolith**: The application's monolithic architecture combined user authentication, product catalogs, shopping cart, checkout, and payment logic in one codebase. Seasonal traffic surges caused CPU and database bottlenecks, making the entire system sluggish or offline.
- **Decision to Break Down Services**: Leadership mandated faster iteration and better uptime, prompting a transition to microservices. The monolith was gradually split into "Product Service," "User Profile Service," "Cart Service," "Inventory/Stock Service," and "Payment Service."
- **Mobile Considerations**: The e-commerce app needed to handle large product images, real-time stock checks, and user-specific recommendations. They introduced a specialized aggregator gateway for the mobile client to reduce round trips.

Key Architecture Highlights

1. **Polyglot Persistence**:
   - **Product Service** used Elasticsearch for flexible text search and fast category browsing.
   - **Cart Service** used Redis for ephemeral session data, supporting quick updates.
   - **Order/Payment** used a relational database for ACID transactions.
2. **Global CDN**: All product images and static content were offloaded to a CDN, drastically reducing bandwidth usage on core microservices.
3. **Autoscaling**: Kubernetes-based deployments ran in three major regions (US-East, EU-West, APAC). A global load balancer routed mobile traffic based on user location, cutting latency by over 40%.
4. **Observability**:
   - **Prometheus** collected metrics (e.g., p95 latency, CPU usage), integrated with **Grafana** dashboards for each microservice.
   - Distributed tracing with **Jaeger** uncovered slow database queries during peak hours, leading to database sharding.
5. **Peak Season Strategies**:
   - **Circuit Breakers** protected Payment and Inventory from cascading failures if the 3rd-party payment gateway slowed.
   - **Bulkheads** in the Notification Service ensured promotional push notifications did not starve mission-critical order flows.

Outcome and Results

- **Reduced Downtimes**: During subsequent seasonal sales, the e-commerce platform scaled up from 10 to 50 microservice replicas for certain services. Shoppers experienced minimal slowdowns, improving brand reputation.

- **Faster Feature Rollouts**: Teams updated or fixed specific microservices without halting the entire system. The mobile app introduced new features (e.g., AR-based product previews) without needing a complete backend redeploy.
- **Lessons Learned**:
  - Data consistency was tricky across distributed services. The team embraced eventual consistency for read-heavy features, offset by ensuring strong consistency in critical payment workflows.
  - Thorough integration and performance tests were essential to catch cross-service bottlenecks.

11.1.2 On-Demand Service Platforms: Handling Real-Time Driver Tracking

Company Profile: A ride-sharing startup offering a **mobile app** for real-time driver tracking and ride dispatch. Millions of daily active users across multiple cities, with varying network conditions and device capabilities.

Legacy Issues Pre-Microservices

- **Monolithic System**: All location tracking, driver matching, and payment logic was jammed into a single node-based service.
- **Scaling Bottlenecks**: Repeatedly, the location-tracking module would saturate CPU usage when thousands of drivers updated position in real time. Any slowdown there impacted the entire app's performance.
- **Slow Releases**: Releasing new driver features required a full redeployment, causing frequent outages or rollback pains.

Microservice Transition

1. **Location Service**: Dedicated microservice handling geospatial indexing, leveraging a specialized NoSQL store (e.g., Redis with geospatial extensions or a purpose-built geolocation database).
2. **Matching/Dispatch Service**: Focused on the logic of pairing riders with nearby drivers, scaling horizontally under load.
3. **Payment Service**: Owned payment methods, fare calculation, and external gateway calls, isolated from geospatial data.
4. **Notification Service**: Sent push notifications for ride confirmations or driver arrivals, integrated with FCM (Firebase Cloud Messaging) and APNs for Apple.

Technical Highlights:

- **Stream Processing**: The location service ingested driver coordinates through Kafka to handle bursts efficiently. A consumer group updated geospatial data with near-real-time indexing.
- **Synchronous vs. Asynchronous**: The matching service used synchronous calls to the location service for current driver positions but also published asynchronous events when a match was found to the Payment and Notification services.
- **Mobile Constraints**:
  - Offline scenarios or low connectivity were mitigated by caching partial data on the device.
  - Frequent driver updates triggered network load, so they introduced a dynamic throttling system that adjusted driver update frequency based on concurrency and user demand.

Outcomes:

- **Scalability**: Handled triple the prior load with fewer disruptions. Real-time tracking remained responsive even in peak commuter hours.
- **Reduced Coupling**: Payment outages or third-party gateway slowdowns no longer blocked ride matching or location updates.
- **Lessons Learned**:
  - Observability was paramount; distributed tracing quickly pinpointed if location indexing or matching logic caused slowdowns.
  - Thorough chaos engineering tests validated partial connectivity scenarios.

11.1.3 Lessons from Social Media and Streaming

Company Profile: A social media platform evolving to incorporate streaming features—live video, ephemeral stories, chat, and push notifications. Their mobile app user base soared from 1 million to 20 million monthly active users within a year.

Challenges and Microservices Adoption

- **Feature Overload**: The original system grew unwieldy with feed algorithms, real-time chat, video transcoding, and user profiles all in one monolith.
- **Heavy Multimedia**: Video streaming required a specialized pipeline for encoding, distributing, and caching, distinct from feed or chat logic.
- **Push Notifications**: Millions of push events per hour triggered by likes, comments, or new livestreams.

Microservice Breakdown:

1. **Feed Service**: Generated personalized timelines using user relationships from a graph database.
2. **Chat Service**: Leveraged WebSockets for real-time messaging, horizontally scaled with a persistent store for chat histories.
3. **Video Service**: Responsible for transcoding, storing, and streaming videos; integrated with a CDN for distribution.
4. **Notification Service**: Focused on push dispatch to APNs/FCM, with dedicated scaling to handle bursts.

Architectural Details:

- **Service Mesh** with mTLS to secure internal calls, ensuring data confidentiality.
- **Caching**:
  - Redis served frequently requested feed segments.
  - The video microservice used an object store (like S3) plus an edge CDN for large media, drastically reducing core service load.
- **AI/ML Integration**: A separate recommendation engine microservice used TensorFlow Serving for personalized content. The feed microservice asynchronously pulled recommended posts.

Outcome:

- **User Engagement** soared as feature releases accelerated—video streaming, ephemeral stories, and chat updates shipped monthly.
- **Operational Complexity** was high: the team introduced chaos engineering to preempt multi-service meltdown scenarios.
- **Key Takeaway**:
  - Clear domain boundaries (chat vs. feed vs. video) improved maintainability.
  - Edge computing/CDN integration was essential for smooth streaming experiences on mobile devices.

11.2 Common Lessons Learned from Real Implementations

11.2.1 Embracing Domain-Driven Boundaries

Across e-commerce, on-demand, and social platforms, a consistent lesson emerges: **domain-driven microservices** that encapsulate distinct functionalities (e.g., "Inventory," "DriverMatching," "VideoTranscoding") are more successful than arbitrary splits. This alignment:

- **Simplifies Ownership**: Each team clearly "owns" one microservice domain.
- **Minimizes Coupling**: Changes remain localized. The Payment team doesn't break the Notification service with a schema tweak.

11.2.2 Scalable Data Management

Persistent data is often a bottleneck. Effective real-world approaches:

- **Polyglot Persistence**: Choosing data stores per domain. For instance, a ridesharing location service might use a geospatial database, while a social feed might use a graph store.
- **Event-Driven Sync**: Many companies rely on asynchronous events to update caches or replicate data, accepting eventual consistency for non-critical operations.

11.2.3 Observability as a First-Class Citizen

In large mobile microservices, partial failures or slowdowns can be notoriously hard to diagnose without:

- **Distributed Tracing**: Tools like Jaeger, Zipkin, or OpenTelemetry to track requests from entry to exit.
- **Structured Logging** and **Log Aggregation**: Centralizing logs across ephemeral containers.
- **Fine-Grained Metrics**: CPU, memory, RPS, p95 latency, error rates, and business metrics (e.g., "orders placed per minute").

In real-world setups, ignoring observability early often leads to firefighting later.

11.2.4 Handling Mobile-Specific Factors

1. **Burst Traffic**: Push notifications can quickly funnel a deluge of requests. Microservices must auto-scale or load shed gracefully.
2. **Offline Support**: E-commerce or messaging apps frequently cache data client-side. The backend microservices must handle eventually consistent writes upon reconnection.
3. **API Versioning**: Because mobile apps aren't always updated promptly, older versions may remain active for months. Backward-compatible contracts or phased deprecation processes are crucial.

11.2.5 Team Culture and DevOps

Shifting to microservices for mobile often requires:

- **Cross-Functional Squads**: Each squad owns a domain microservice, from design to deployment.
- **Automated CI/CD**: Comprehensive test suites, canary rollouts, and quick rollback strategies reduce the risk of frequent releases.
- **Avoiding Microservices Sprawl**: Over-splitting leads to "nano-services" with excessive overhead. Real companies often pivot back to fewer or more carefully sized services after initial fragmentation.

11.3 Emerging Trends

11.3.1 AI and ML Integration in Microservices

As personalization, recommendations, and real-time analytics become standard in mobile apps, microservices are increasingly hosting **AI/ML models**:

1. **Inference as a Service**: A dedicated ML microservice loads a trained model (e.g., TensorFlow, PyTorch) for tasks like image classification, language translation, or recommendation scoring. Mobile apps send data to the ML service, receiving predictions in real time.
2. **Edge ML**: Some advanced setups push certain model inference to the device itself (e.g., Apple's Core ML or Android's ML Kit). The microservices handle model updates or fallback for more complex tasks.
3. **Model Versioning**: MLOps pipelines store multiple model versions, A/B testing new ones. Microservices must manage backward compatibility for older models if the mobile client's features rely on them.

Key Considerations:

- **Latency**: Large model inference might be CPU/GPU-intensive. Some companies rely on GPUs or TPUs in data centers for complex tasks. Others opt for edge-based or simplified on-device models.
- **Data Privacy**: With user data used for ML, ensure compliance with GDPR or local data regulations. Possibly anonymize or aggregate data before sending to ML microservices.

11.3.2 5G and Edge Computing Influences

The rollout of **5G networks** and widespread edge infrastructure (e.g., telco providers hosting mini data centers near towers) can drastically reduce network latency and bandwidth constraints for mobile devices.

Potential shifts:

- **More Frequent Interactions**: With higher speeds, apps can offload more logic to the cloud. Microservices might see a surge in request volume, meaning architectures must be ready for double or triple the RPS.
- **Real-Time AR/VR**: Low latency is crucial for augmented reality or gaming features. Microservices near the edge can supply position-based data with minimal round-trip time.
- **Distributed Mini Clusters**: In some future scenarios, each major city could host a micro-Kubernetes cluster for local traffic processing, replicating or syncing with main data centers asynchronously.

11.3.3 Event-Driven and Serverless Microservices

Microservices are also evolving:

- **Serverless**: Functions as a Service (e.g., AWS Lambda, Google Cloud Functions) can complement or replace always-on containers, particularly for unpredictable or spiky workloads, saving cost.
- **Event-Driven Patterns**: Many real-time mobile features (push notifications, analytics) rely on pub/sub or streaming platforms. Tools like Apache Kafka, RabbitMQ, or cloud pub/sub services reduce tight coupling and handle ephemeral usage bursts.
- **Stateful Serverless**: Emerging frameworks combine serverless with ephemeral state or durable state stores, further simplifying microservices that need short-term data retention.

11.3.4 Security and Compliance in a Global Context

As data privacy laws (GDPR, CCPA, HIPAA, PCI-DSS, etc.) proliferate, microservices must handle user data with extreme care. Key future directions:

- **Zero-Trust Networking**: Automatic mutual TLS enforced at the service mesh layer.
- **Privacy by Design**: Minimizing data collection on mobile, encrypting end-to-end, and providing user-level data controls.
- **Blockchain for Data Auditing**: Some organizations experiment with immutable ledgers for critical transactions or compliance audits. While not mainstream, the desire for verifiable data history might drive more advanced cryptographic approaches.

11.4 Long-Term Maintenance and Evolution

11.4.1 Refactoring or Replacing Services Over Time

Microservices are rarely static. Over years, domain models shift, technologies evolve, and original service boundaries may no longer make sense. **Refactoring** can involve:

1. **Merging Nano-Services**: If teams realize a service boundary was too granular. Combining them can simplify communications and overhead.
2. **Splitting Overgrown Services**: Alternatively, if a microservice becomes a "mini-monolith" with 50 endpoints, it might be time to carve out a separate domain.
3. **Upgrading Tech Stacks**: A service originally built in Node.js might be migrated to Go for concurrency benefits. Another might shift from a relational DB to NoSQL for scaling.

Challenges:

- **Coordinated Migrations**: Dependent microservices might rely on old data schemas or endpoints. Feature flags, versioning, or parallel runs mitigate disruptions.
- **Maintaining Backward Compatibility**: Mobile apps that haven't updated might still use older endpoints, requiring transitional code or "translation layers."

11.4.2 Migrating to New Platforms and Technologies

Fashions in technology change rapidly:

- **Container Orchestrators**: Some organizations pivot from self-managed Kubernetes to fully managed cloud solutions (e.g., EKS, GKE, AKS) or to serverless container platforms (e.g., Fargate, Cloud Run).
- **Service Mesh Evolution**: Tools like Istio, Linkerd, or Consul might get replaced or upgraded, requiring a controlled rollout.
- **Emerging Runtimes**: Some microservices might adopt **WebAssembly (Wasm)** for safe, portable execution, especially relevant if you want to unify server, edge, and client logic.

Best Practices:

- **Gradual Rollouts**: Migrate one microservice at a time, or run new and old infrastructure in parallel, carefully shifting traffic.
- **Infrastructure as Code**: Tools like Terraform or Pulumi can codify the entire environment, ensuring reproducible migrations.
- **Testing**: Comprehensive tests (unit, integration, contract, E2E) are indispensable for confident migrations.

11.4.3 Monitoring and Observability as Systems Evolve

As microservices grow, the volume of logs, metrics, and traces can skyrocket. Maintaining cost-effective and actionable observability requires:

- **Sampling**: Only collecting full traces for a fraction of requests or for error conditions.
- **Intelligent Log Retention**: Tier older logs or set time-based retention.
- **Machine Learning**: Some advanced observability platforms analyze patterns or anomalies.

Continuous Reevaluation: Observability architectures must be revisited every few quarters to handle new scale, new data types, or new regulations around data retention.

11.5 Looking Ahead

11.5.1 Convergence of Mobile, Edge, and AI

Over the next few years, we might see an even tighter interplay among **mobile devices**, **edge computing**, and **ML-driven microservices**:

- **More "Smart" Microservices**: Almost every user-facing interaction might rely on some machine learning predictions, from auto-suggestions to personalized UIs.
- **High-Fidelity Streaming**: Video, AR, and VR experiences become more common as 5G and Wi-Fi 6 reduce latency. Microservices that handle real-time sensor data or video processing may run at the edge for immediate user feedback.
- **Device-Cloud Synergy**: Some logic moves client-side (faster responses, privacy), while heavy computation or aggregated data tasks remain in microservices. This dynamic partitioning evolves as device capabilities grow.

11.5.2 Service Meshes and Zero-Trust by Default

In modern microservices, manual configurations for mutual TLS or per-service ACLs can be tedious. We can anticipate:

- **Service Mesh Defaults**: Tools might automatically generate certificates, apply network policies, and route traffic without explicit developer effort.
- **Security as a Commodity**: Deploying a new microservice might come with default security posture (TLS, logs, metrics) from day one.
- **Runtime Threat Detection**: Built-in intrusion detection or anomaly detection at the mesh layer could mitigate attacks quickly.

11.5.3 Microservices Governance and Organizational Impact

Microservices are as much about organizational structure as they are about technology. Future developments may push:

- **Decentralized Governance**: Each squad remains autonomous, choosing languages or frameworks. But over time, standard practices (e.g., shared libraries for logging, consistent monitoring) might become mandatory as complexity grows.
- **Platform Engineering**: Internal platform teams create self-service tools for microservice deployment, secrets management, and load balancing, letting dev squads focus on domain logic.
- **AI-Assisted Development**: Tools might auto-suggest service boundaries or generate migration plans from monolith code. They may also recommend test coverage gaps or optimum caching strategies.

Final Reflections: Synthesis of Microservices for Mobile

Throughout this book, the chapters have illuminated:

- **Design Fundamentals** (Chapters 1–3): Why microservices matter in mobile contexts, with key architectural principles and domain-driven design.
- **Data Management** (Chapters 4–5): Communication patterns, asynchronous flows, data partitioning, caching, and more.
- **Deployment, Infrastructure, Observability, Security** (Chapters 6–8): Ensuring robust, maintainable operations.
- **Performance, Scalability, Testing** (Chapters 9–10): Techniques for handling surges in mobile traffic, optimizing microservices, and guaranteeing quality.
- **Case Studies and Future Outlook** (this chapter): Real successes, pitfalls, and evolving trends.

www.ingramcontent.com/pod-product-compliance
Lightning Source LLC
LaVergne TN
LVHW080117070326
832902LV00015B/2631